IN THE SPOTLIGHT

We use our creativity to reach an audience.

SCHOLASTIC

LITERACY PLACE®

Copyright acknowledgments and credits appear on page 136, which constitutes an extension of this copyright page.

5 6 7 8 9 10   24   02 01 00 99 98 97

Attend
an Actor's Workshop

We use our creativity to reach an audience.

Stories to Tell

The stories we tell connect the past to the present.

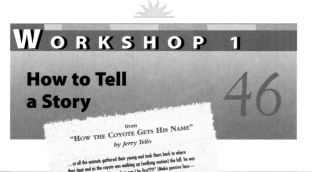

On Stage

Through the performing arts, we entertain others.

VANESSA'S BAD GRADE
by Ross Brown
Scene Five
Vanessa is in her room when Theo walks in.
VANESSA: I got my history test back.
(She hands him the test paper.)
THEO: Whoa. This is a "D."
VANESSA: I know. I've never gotten a "D" before. I've seen them, but never next to my name.
THEO: And this one is in red. That's the worst kind to get.
VANESSA: I don't know how it happened. Robert and I studied for this.

Speak Out

Speeches help us persuade and inform others.

Trade Books

The following books accompany this *In the Spotlight* SourceBook.

**Dear Dr. Bell ...
Your Friend,
Helen Keller**

by Judith
St. George

Fiction

**Koya DeLaney
and the Good
Girl Blues**

by Eloise
Greenfield

AWARD WINNING
Author

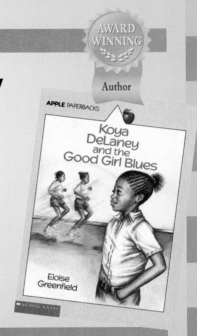

Fiction

School Spirit

by Johanna
Hurwitz

AWARD WINNING
Author

Nonfiction

**That's a Wrap:
How Movies
Are Made**

by Ned Dowd
photographed
by Henry
Horenstein

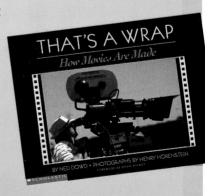

Stories to Tell

Join a young girl
and her friends
as they listen to
real-life stories on
a neighbor's porch.

Read a Chinese
tale about a
strange encounter
in the forest. Meet
three spellbinding
storytellers.

WORKSHOP 1

Tell a story of your own or one
that you've heard before.

from
"HOW THE COYOTE GETS HIS NAME"
by Jerry Tello

...so all the animals gathered their young and took them back to where
they slept and as the coyote was walking up (walking motion) the hill, he was
thinking, "How can I be first...how can I be first?!?!" (Make pensive face—
look at extended finger.)
By this time, the Sun (look up) had finished his cycle and touched
(tap-on-the-shoulder motion with index finger) the Moon on the shoulder and
Ms. Moon began sharing her brilliance.
And there sat (sitting action) the coyote on top of the hill, under a tree,
still thinking how he could be first (index finger to temple, as if thinking), when
he had a brilliant idea!
(Eyes wide, mouth open). "I'll just stay up all night!" That way, I'll see Mr.

FROM MISS IDA'S PORCH

by SANDRA BELTON

illustrated by FLOYD COOPER

AWARD WINNING

Illustrator

$\mathcal{T}$here's a very best time of day on Church Street. My street. It begins when the sky and my feelings match, both kind of rosy around the edges.

You can hear all the best-time noises—Shoo Kate and Mr. Fisher laughing from their kitchen. Reginald and T-Bone slamming out their back door. Mr. Porter coming home from work in his noisy ole car, calling out to everybody he passes on the street. Netta practicing on her piano (mostly to get out of washing dinner dishes), and Mr. Willie making his just-checkin'-on call to Mrs. Jackson, his ninety-year-old mama.

The noises feel good.

Most of the big kids are getting ready to hang out somewhere, like at the drugstore down on the corner, or on the steps in front of the church. Those are some of their favorite pretending places—the boys pretending not to see the girls, and the girls pretending to ignore the boys. . . . Like my sister Sylvia pretending to ignore Peewee.

Most of the little kids are getting ready to get ready for bed. Getting ready for bed takes a long time for the little kids. Some of them can make it last all the way to the end of the best time. Especially the Tolver kids.

"Just five more minutes, Mama, please!" they say. Then after five minutes they hide somewhere in the yard for five more minutes. Then they start pleading all over again for five more minutes.

But most of the kids on Church Street are in-between kids. Like Freda and me.

Some of the best times we just sit on her porch or mine, playing jacks or reading comics. Sometimes we play statues with Rosetta and Punkin and Rodney. Sometimes T-Bone plays, too.

Most of the best times, though, just about all of us end up at Miss Ida's. Sitting on her porch.

Miss Ida's house is halfway down Church Street. That's probably one reason folks end up there a lot. Another reason is Miss Ida herself. She and the best time are kind of alike. Soft, peaceful.

But the biggest reason we all end up there is that Miss Ida's porch is a telling place.

⚜

Usually Mr. Fisher comes over to sit on the porch about the same time we do. It's about the time the sky is getting rosy all over. You know then that the best time is settling in.

Miss Ida calls Mr. Fisher "Poissant" because they both come from Louisiana, and that's what people there used to call him.

Mr. Fisher has been all over. It's hard to tell how old he is. But from all the stuff he's done, he could be really old. He doesn't look old at all, though. Especially when he walks. He sorta bounces. Miss Ida always says, "Poissant has a jaunty step."

Mr. Fisher has lots of memories about the places he's been and things he's seen. Almost *anything* can make him think about something he saw or heard or did a while back. He'll start out, "Puts my mind on the time . . . ," and we know what's coming.

"Tell us about that time, Poissant," Miss Ida will say to Mr. Fisher when he begins his remembering.

And he will.

Like the time Freda and Punkin were arguing about what Mrs. Jackson had said when she was over at Punkin's house, visiting Miss Esther, Punkin's aunt.

"Lena Horne ain't never visited Miz Jackson, Punkin," Freda said. "Miz Jackson was just talking outta her head, girl. You know she ninety years old. You crazy for believing her."

"You don't know nothing, Freda." Punkin was getting angry. "Just 'cause Miz Jackson's ninety don't mean she talking outta her head. Most time Miz Jackson make more sense than you!"

Punkin and T-Bone almost fell over laughing. Me, too. And this made Freda fighting mad.

"Hold on there, Miss Lady," said Mr. Fisher, taking hold of one of Freda's hands. "Don't press ugly on that pretty face. Tell me now, how come you think Lena Horne couldn't have stayed at Mrs. Jackson's house?"

"'Cause Lena Horne is famous. Why would she want to stay at Miz Jackson's?"

"Why not?" Mr. Fisher settled back in his chair.

I had a feeling that some remembering was getting started.

Used to be that most all the famous black folks who came to town stayed at somebody's house."

"How come, Mr. Fisher?" Freda sat on the stoop in front of Mr. Fisher.

"Nowhere else for them to stay! Couldn't stay in hotels. Hotels didn't allow no black guests! Famous or not. When our folk came to town to give a speech, put on a show, or whatever they came to do, we had to be the ones to give 'em a bed.

"Puts my mind on a time back in thirty-nine. I was working in West Virginia then. Working in the mines. Lived in a nice town close to where I worked. Lots of good folks there, working hard to make a life for themselves and their children."

Mr. Fisher's remembering was making him smile.

"Anyhow, a big dance took place in the town every year. Folks came from all around to go to this dance. That year, 1939, the dance was *really* going to be special. Duke Ellington was coming to town. The great bandsman himself was coming to play for the dance."

"Was Duke Ellington famous?" I bet none of us knew who Duke Ellington was. Punkin was brave enough to ask.

Mr. Fisher almost jumped out of his chair. "Don't they teach you children nothin' in school? Duke Ellington *famous*?" Mr. Fisher was almost shouting.

"Don't get bothered now, Poissant." Miss Ida put her hand on Mr. Fisher's arm. She was speaking in that peaceful way she has.

"Can't expect anybody to listen if you shouting, now can you," said Miss Ida. "Just tell the children about Duke Ellington. Tell them about the sound of that band. A sound that made your feet get a life of their own on the dance floor. Tell them how he not only led the band from his piano but also wrote most of the songs they played. How you could hum your little baby to sleep with some of those pretty songs. And how some of those songs were played by big orchestras and sung by huge choirs in halls all over the world."

Mr. Fisher had a big smile on his face. "I ain't got to tell them, Miss Ida. You doin' a fine job, a mighty fine job!"

The sky was starting to look like the never-tell blue blanket on Big Mama's bed. "Never-tell blue is light enough to still be blue but dark enough to hide the dirt," Big Mama says.

The best-time noises were still there, but they had changed. You could hear the chirping bugs. One of the Tolver kids was crying. Probably asking for something he couldn't have. Mr. Willie was playing his radio. Jazz.

Mr. Fisher was still remembering.

"Yessir. The great Duke Ellington was coming to play for us, for our dance, and there was not one hotel in the state that would put him up and take his money for doin' it. If he had a mind to rest himself in a bed, it was goin' have to be in the home of some black person."

"Did he stay with you, Mr. Fisher?" Punkin asked.

"Not with me, exactly, but in the house where I was living. Mrs. Lomax's house. Mrs. Lomax had a big, fine house, and she kept it real nice. I rented a room on the third floor."

Mr. Fisher started to grin. Like he always did when he got to a part he liked to tell.

"I was there when the great man arrived with three of his bandsmen."

"So you got to meet Duke Ellington?" T-Bone was impressed. We all were.

"I not only met him, I was there when he sat at the piano in Mrs. Lomax's parlor. Duke's playing heated up that little room. I'm telling you it did. He was some kinda good!"

Mr. Fisher grew quiet. A remembering quiet. He stopped smiling, too.

"Humph. Imagine that. A man like that. Talented, famous, everything! Not being able to pay his *own* money to sleep in a crummy little hotel room, just because he was black."

After that we were all quiet. I was wishing I knew more about what Mr. Fisher was remembering. I bet Freda was wishing so, too.

venin', everybody. Must be some powerful thinking over here tonight, 'cause everybody's deep into it."

Shoo Kate was climbing the steps to the porch. I hadn't even heard her coming up the walk. Nobody else must have either.

"Hey, Shoo Kate. Come over here by me." Miss Ida patted the place on the swing beside her.

Shoo Kate is Mr. Fisher's wife. Her name is really Mrs. Kate Fisher, but just about everybody calls her Shoo Kate. She told us one time that when she was little she used to tease her baby brother, telling him that their mama said he had to call her Sugar Kate 'cause she was so sweet. The name came out Shoo Kate when her baby brother said it. Then everybody started calling her that. She even told us kids to call her Shoo Kate instead of Mrs. Fisher.

After she sat down Shoo Kate reached over and poked Mr. Fisher. "What you been telling these folks, Fisher, to make everybody so quiet?"

"I ain't been tellin' them nothing you don't already know, darlin'." Mr. Fisher and Shoo Kate smiled at each other. They always seemed to be smiling and laughing together.

"Did any famous people stay in your house, Shoo Kate?" T-bone asked.

"Now I know what talking's been over here," Shoo Kate said, laughing. "Fisher, you been telling them about that time Duke Ellington came and stayed at the place in West Virginia where you were living."

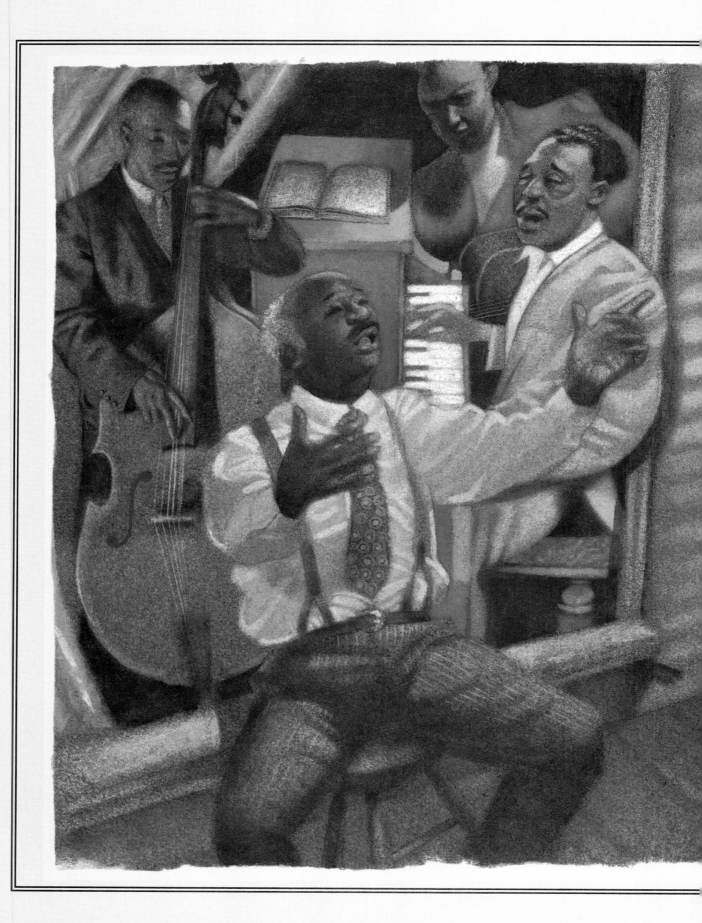

"I sure was," said Mr. Fisher. "No reason to keep that fine bit of history a secret."

"So it's history now, is it, Poissant," said Miss Ida. I think she was teasing. All the grown-ups laughed.

"Well, T," said Shoo Kate, "I never made history like Fisher here, but I *was* somewhere one time when history was being made."

"Shoo Kate, I bet I know what you're talking about. Go on, tell the children." Miss Ida sounded excited.

The sky was really getting dark. I like the best time most of all when the sky is dark. You can imagine that almost anything is out there. You can imagine almost anything.

Shoo Kate began her story.

"Around the same time Fisher was living in West Virginia, I was living with my family in Washington, D.C. My papa worked for the railroad. He was a train-car porter, so he had to travel most of the time. All of us looked forward to Papa's days off, the days he was going to be home.

"Oh, those were the best days—the days when Papa was home. He made sure we all did something special on those days. All of us together, Papa, Mama, and each one of us kids. We didn't have much money, but we had enough. And as shut out as we were in Washington, we could still find lots of things to do."

"What do you mean 'shut out,' Shoo Kate?" Freda asked.

"Just what the words say, sugar. Black folks were shut out.

We couldn't go to the movie theaters, the big restaurants, just about anyplace you think folks ought to be able to go if the place is open to the public and folks have the inclination to go. Why, when my papa was growing up in Washington, black folks couldn't even go to the national monuments!"

Punkin looked at Shoo Kate kind of funny. "But Washington is the capital city," she said. "That's where they make laws for the whole country. How could they break the law, keeping folks from going places just 'cause they was black?"

Freda had been waiting all evening to get back at Punkin, and her chance had finally come.

"Now look who's talking outta her head! Girl, don't you know nothing? Used to be that the *law* said it was okay to keep black folks out," she said.

"Don't you two get started now. Freda's right about the laws, of course," Miss Ida said, pulling Punkin down to sit beside her. "But that's another story. A long story for another time. Go on, Shoo Kate, please."

❧

Shoo Kate did.

"Anyhow, this one time we were all real excited because Papa was going to be home for Easter. He wasn't always able to be there for holidays. So we were all looking forward to having him home and being able to dress up in our new clothes and go to church together.

"But it wasn't Papa's plan for us to go to church that Easter Sunday. After we were all dressed and ready to leave the house, Papa said we were going to catch the trolley car.

"Then we really got excited. Catching the trolley car! We knew that Papa must be planning something special because we didn't need to catch the trolley to go to our church. We only had to walk a couple of blocks to get there."

Shoo Kate sat up straighter. It was like her remembering was pushing at her back.

"How grand we were, riding on the trolley that Easter Sunday morning. And even grander when Papa explained that we were on our way to the Lincoln Memorial. That was exciting enough. Then he went on to tell us that we were going there to hear one of the greatest voices in America!"

"Who were you going to hear, Shoo Kate?" Freda asked the question this time.

"We were going to hear Marian Anderson. A grand, grand singer—a voice more magnificent than you could *ever* imagine!

"But there was more to it than just going to hear Marian Anderson sing. Much more."

Shoo Kate wiggled down to the edge of her chair and moved her face closer to us.

"It was like this. Several months before that Easter Sunday, a concert had been arranged. It was arranged for Marian Anderson to sing at Constitution Hall. Constitution Hall was the big concert stage in Washington, where all the famous musicians appeared. People from all over the world.

"Marian Anderson was certainly famous. *And* she had sung all over the world. Didn't matter, though. Marian Anderson's concert was not going to take place in Constitution Hall. You see, Marian Anderson was black. The people who owned the hall said no black musician was going to perform on their stage!"

Shoo Kate sat back in her chair. Her eyes got narrow.

"While we rode on the trolley, Papa told us what had happened. A lot of people in Washington were furious about Miss Anderson not being able to sing at Constitution Hall. The wife of the president of the United States was one of these furious people. So she and some others got together to arrange for Miss Anderson to sing somewhere else."

Shoo Kate started moving her hands as she talked. Her smile started coming back.

"Constitution Hall with its white columns and high-up ceiling wouldn't welcome Marian Anderson. But the Lincoln Memorial would! There would be no walls to keep people out. And the sky would be the ceiling! On Easter Sunday morning just about anybody who wanted to would be able to hear and *see* Marian Anderson sing. Including my entire family!"

Shoo Kate's smile was all over her face.

"At first we thought it might rain. We had gotten there early, very early, hoping to get close enough to see. While we waited, we kept looking up at the sky, wishing for the sun to come out.

"The crowd grew and grew. So many people, all kinds of people. Black folks, white folks, standing there together in front of the Lincoln Memorial, waiting to hear Marian Anderson sing."

Mr. Fisher started grinning himself. What Shoo Kate was about to say must have been his favorite part of the story.

"It was time for the concert to start. Then, just as Marian Anderson was getting ready to walk out onto the place she was gonna sing from, the sun came out. Yes, it did!"

Shoo Kate's voice grew softer. So soft we moved closer to hear her.

"When the concert started, our papa took turns holding the little ones up so they could get a better look. When he reached down to get my baby brother Jimmy, I saw tears rolling down his cheeks.

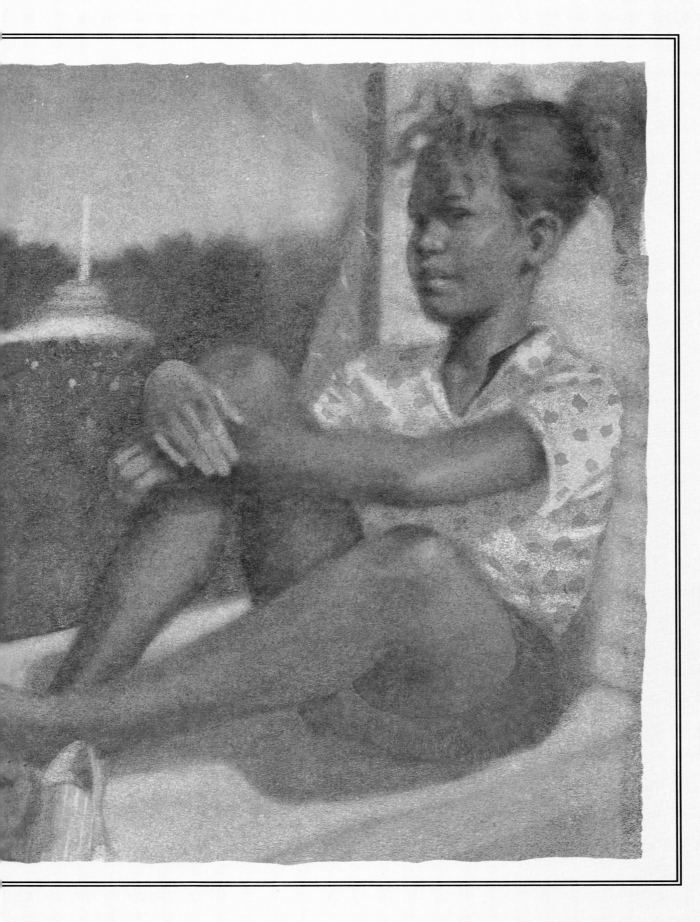

"I asked my mama if Papa was crying 'cause he was happy. This is what Mama said to us sometimes when we caught her crying. Mama said that some of Papa's tears were happy tears, but some were not. Some were tears of sadness, and maybe even anger.

"Mama said to me, 'Listen to the words she sings, Kate.' Miss Anderson was singing a song I knew, 'My Country, 'Tis of Thee.' I recognized the words:

> '. . . *From every mountainside*
> *Let freedom ring*'

" 'Your papa's thinking about those words and what they should mean,' Mama said. 'Thoughts like that might be making him feel good and bad at the same time. That's probably why there are tears on your papa's face.' "

Shoo Kate sat back in her chair. Her voice got almost regular.

"So you see, on that Easter Sunday I saw history being made there at the Lincoln Memorial. I also saw my papa cry with pride and sadness at the same time. It was a day that will live in my memory forever."

Shoo Kate's remembering had kind of put a spell on us. On everybody listening. Even Punkin was real still, and she was usually moving around like a doll on strings. When my father and my sister Sylvia walked up on the porch, we all jumped. Nobody had heard them coming.

"Goodness, you all gave me a fright." Miss Ida got up. "Hi, Sylvia. Here, take my seat, J.S.," she said to Daddy. "I'll get more chairs from the house."

"No need, Ida," Daddy said. "A few folks are going to be leaving very soon and there'll be plenty of room."

Daddy looked over at me and Freda. I knew that the very best time was about to be over for us.

"Hey, J.S., what you been up to?" Daddy and Mr. Fisher were shaking hands.

"I just been walking down to the corner to make sure Sylvia and her friends know it's time to come home."

"Sylvia don't know nothing when Peewee's around." I just had to say that. My sister thinks she's something special just 'cause bony ole Peewee said she was cute.

"Shut up!" Sylvia wanted to hit me. I just knew it.

"Don't speak that way to your sister," Daddy said to Sylvia. "And you, missy," he said pointing to me, "if you want to get your extra few minutes here, I think you'd better have kinder thoughts for Sylvia."

"There's been some wonderful thoughts on this porch tonight, folks. Let's keep the good words going." Miss Ida always makes things okay.

"J.S.," she said, "you missed a wonderful story. Shoo Kate was telling us about the time she saw Marian Anderson."

"Oh, yeah," Daddy said, like he was remembering something. "You told me a little about that, Shoo Kate. I wish I had been here to hear the whole story."

"Tell him the story, Shoo Kate. We'd love to hear it again. Right, Freda?" I wanted so much to make the best time last.

"Good try, baby, but it won't work tonight." Daddy hardly ever let my tricks work on him.

"I have another chapter for that story, however. Want to hear it?" While he was talking, Daddy winked at Shoo Kate. I thought he was fooling.

Miss Ida sat up in her seat. Like she felt the same as me. Wanting the evening to go on.

"Come on, J.S., sit down and take your turn this evening." Miss Ida motioned for us to make room for Daddy.

Then my daddy started his remembering.

I had an uncle—Uncle Henry—who lived in Washington," Daddy began. "He taught at Howard University there, for many years.

"Uncle Henry was a big man, well over six feet tall. He had wide, full eyebrows that came together like a hairy *V* whenever he frowned. And Uncle Henry frowned easily. Especially when one of us was messin' up. His voice was like a drum—booming, deep.

"His voice, his frown, and his attitude could put the fear of God in you. Uncle Henry didn't play!"

Daddy chuckled.

"I dearly loved Uncle Henry, though. We all did. In fact, he was probably the favorite of everybody in the family. Whenever there was going to be a family gathering, we all wanted it to be at Uncle Henry's. At Uncle Henry's you knew there would be lots to do, lots to eat, and best of all, lots and lots of Uncle Henry."

Daddy has a deep voice, too. A good telling voice.

"Uncle Henry had worked hard to get where he wanted to be in life. And he was one of the lucky ones: He got there. Yep, Uncle Henry was a grand old guy. One of those people you hope will go on forever."

Daddy looked out into the darkness. I think he was seeing Uncle Henry in his mind. I think I was, too.

"Whenever us nephews and nieces were gathered around the breakfast or dinner table, Uncle Henry would claim the floor, but we didn't mind at all. Uncle Henry was a magnificent storyteller! And though we didn't know it then, his stories were like fuel for our young minds.

"Uncle Henry firmly believed that the knowledge of our history—the history of black folks—was the most important story that we could ever be told. I can just hear him now: 'You can know where you are going in this world only if you know where you've been!'"

Mr. Fisher slapped his hand on his leg. "Now that's a man after my own heart!" he said.

"*Shhhhh*, Fisher. Let J.S. go on," Shoo Kate said.

Daddy did. "Uncle Henry held us spellbound with his stories. He told us about the great civilizations of Africa that existed thousands of years ago, and—"

"Tell us about that!" T-Bone moved real close to Daddy.

"That's a story for another time, T," Daddy said. "I'll be sure to tell you, but I'd better get on with this one now.

"One of Uncle Henry's stories described how he had been there that Easter Sunday at the Lincoln Memorial. But that same story had another part, a part that told something that had happened *before* that famous Sunday.

"You see, another important event had taken place in that same spot seventeen years earlier—the dedication of the Lincoln Memorial. Uncle Henry had been there then, too."

"Wow!" said T-Bone and Punkin. I knew how they felt.

"It wasn't as much of a 'wow' as you might think, kids. At the dedication of this monument to the man known as the Great Emancipator, the black folks who came had to stand in a special section. A section off to the left of the monument. Away from the white folks, who could stand dead center, right in front."

Daddy had started breathing hard. It sounded loud. Everything else was quiet. Except Daddy's breathing.

"Anyhow, during one of our visits to Uncle Henry, Marian Anderson was going to be giving another concert. It was very important to Uncle Henry that all the nieces and nephews have a chance to go."

"So, you heard a concert at the Lincoln Memorial, too, right?" T-Bone sure was making it hard for Daddy to get on with his story. I wanted to put some tape over his mouth.

Daddy smiled. "No, as a matter of fact, I didn't. The concert I went to was held at Constitution Hall."

"What?" All of us were surprised at this twist.

"That's right," Daddy said. His breathing wasn't so loud now. "It was 1965, over twenty-five years since that concert at the Lincoln Memorial. Marian Anderson was now at the end of her career as a singer. This concert was taking place so she could say farewell to Washington audiences.

"Constitution Hall was still one of the finest concert stages in Washington, a stage now open to all performers, no matter what their color. It had been that way for years. But that concert and that magnificent singer were special. Very special."

Everybody was looking at Daddy as he went on.

"Many of the people in the hall that night were African Americans. Some of these black people had also been standing on the grass under the sky that Easter Sunday morning. And some, like Uncle Henry, had been out there on the grass for the dedication in 1922. Now these same people were sitting in the forbidden hall, some of them in the best seats in the house!

"When Marian Andersen came onto the stage, the applause of the crowd was like the roar of a thousand pounding seas. It went on and on and on. But above the noise, there was one thing I heard very clearly."

"You heard your Uncle Henry, right?" Miss Ida was smiling at Dad. And her eyes were sparkly. Like raindrops are sparkly when I can look through them on my window and see the sun.

My dad's voice was real soft. "I did, Ida. I could hear Uncle Henry. But I think I would have known what he was saying even if I hadn't heard him. Just like I can hear him right now: 'You can know where you are going in this world only if you know where you've been!'"

In the quiet after Daddy stopped talking, I looked out into the velvet black sky. I tried to imagine the sound of a thousand pounding seas. I tried to imagine some other things, too. Like how it might have been to ride on a trolley. Or to spend the night in the same house with a famous person. Or to go to a famous monument and not be able to stand where I wanted to.

My dad's story brought the end to the very best time that evening.

Like we always did, Freda, T, Punkin, and I said good-night to all the grown-ups and walked each other home. I walked Freda home and then she walked me home, and then I walked her home again. Sylvia told on us like she usually does, so I finally went home for good to go to bed.

Just before I go to sleep is the very, very last part of the very best time. After I'm in bed and my light is turned off, I can look out my bedroom window and see Miss Ida's porch.

Most of the time the grown-ups are still there. I can hear them talking and laughing, but it's soft and far away.

These sounds feel good. They keep the very best times close. So close that they're with me when my eyelids stop cooperating and just drop. I think the very best times go with me into my dreams. . . .

SOURCE

Chinese Folk
Tale Collection

AWARD
WINNING

Book

FROM
The Rainbow People

THE HOME

"The Homecoming," by Laurence Yep, is a story from The Rainbow People, a collection of 20 Chinese folk tales. In this book Yep retells traditional stories that were collected and translated in the 1930s by a researcher who worked with Chinese Americans living in Oakland, California.

Once there was a woodcutter who minded everyone's business but his own. If you were digging a hole, he knew a better way to grip the shovel. If you were cooking a fish, he knew a better recipe. As his village said, he knew a little of everything and most of nothing.

If his wife and children hadn't made palm leaf fans, the family would have starved. Finally his wife got tired of everyone laughing at them. "You're supposed to be a woodcutter. Go up to the hill and cut some firewood."

COMING

by Laurence Yep

illustrations by Chi Chung

"Any fool can do that." The woodcutter picked up his hatchet. "In the mountains there's plenty of tall oak. That's what burns best."

His wife pointed out the window. "But there's a stand of pine just over the ridgetop."

Her husband looked pained. "Pine won't sell as well. I'll take my load into town, where folk are too busy to cut their own. Then I'll come back with loads of cash." With a laugh, he shouldered his long pole. After he cut the wood, he would tie it into two big bundles and place each at the end of the pole. Then he would balance the load on his shoulder.

Waving good-bye to his children, he left their house; but his wife walked right with him. "What are you doing?" he asked.

His wife folded her arms as they walked along. "Escorting you."

He slowed down by a boy who was making a kite out of paper and rice paste. "That thing will never fly. You should—"

His wife caught his arm and pulled him along. "Don't be such a busybody."

"If a neighbor's doing something wrong, it's the charitable thing to set that person straight." He tried to stop by a man who was feeding his ducks. "Say, friend. Those ducks'll get fatter if—"

His wife yanked him away and gave him a good shake. "Do I have to blindfold you? We have two children to feed."

"I'm not lazy," he grumbled.

She kept dragging him out of the village. "I never said you were. You can do the work of two people when no one else is around. You're just too easily distracted."

She went with him to the very edge of the fields and sent him on his way. "Remember," she called after him. "Don't talk to anyone."

He walked with long, steady strides through the wooded hills. "I'll show her. It isn't how often you do something, it's how you do it. I'll cut twice the wood and sell it for double the price and come back in half the time."

Complaining loudly to himself, he moved deep into the mountains. I want just the right sort of oak, he thought to himself. As he walked along, he kept an eye out for a likely tree.

He didn't see the funny old man until he bumped into him. "Oof, watch where you're going," the old man said.

The old man had a head that bulged as big as a melon. He was dressed in a yellow robe embroidered with storks and pine trees.

Playing chess with the old man was another man so fat he could not close his robe. In his hand he had a large fan painted with scenes.

The fat man wagged a finger at the old man. "Don't try to change the subject. I've got you. It's checkmate in two moves."

The funny old man looked back at the chessboard. The lines were a bright red on yellow paper, and the chess pieces were flat disks with words painted in gold on their tops.

"Is it now, is it now?" the funny old man mused.

The woodcutter remembered his wife's warning. But he said to himself, "I'm not actually talking to them. I'm advising them." So he put down his hatchet and pole. "Actually, if you moved that piece"—he jabbed at a disk—"and moved it there"—he pointed at a spot on the board—"you'd have him."

But the old man moved a different disk.

The fat man scratched the top of his bald head. "Now how'd you think of that?"

The woodcutter rubbed his chin. "Yes, how *did* you think of that?" But then he nodded his head and pointed to one of the fat man's disks. "Still, if you shifted that one, you'd win."

However, the fat man ignored him as he made another move.

"Well," the woodcutter said to the old man, "you've got him now."

Bu the old man paid him no more mind than the fat man. "Hmmm," he murmured, and set his chin on his fist as he studied the board.

The woodcutter became so caught up in the game that he squatted down. "I know what you have to do. I'll be right here just in case you need to ask."

Neither man said anything to the woodcutter. They just went on playing, and as they played, the woodcutter became more and more fascinated. He forgot about chopping wood. He even forgot about going home.

When it was night, the funny old man opened a big basket and lifted out a lantern covered with stars. He hung it from a tree and the game went on. Night passed on into day, but the woodcutter was as involved in the game now as the two men.

"Let's take a break." The old man slipped a peach from one big sleeve. The peach was big as the woodcutter's fist, and it filled the woods with a sweet aroma.

"You're just stalling for time," the fat man said. "Move."

"I'm hungry," the old man complained, and took a big bite. However, he shoved a piece along the board. When he held the peach out to the fat man, the fat man bit into it hungrily.

Alternating moves and bites, they went on until there was nothing left of the peach except the peach stone. "I feel much better now," the old man said, and threw the stone over his shoulder.

As the two men had eaten the peach, the woodcutter had discovered that he was famished, but the only thing was the peach stone. "Maybe I can suck on this stone and forget about being hungry. But I wish one of them would ask me for help. We could finish this game a lot quicker."

He tucked the stone into his mouth and tasted some of the peach juices. Instantly, he felt himself filled with energy. Goodness, he thought, I feel like there were lightning bolts zipping around inside me. And he went on watching the game with new energy.

After seven days, the old man stopped and stretched. "I think we're going to have to call this game a draw."

The fat man sighed. "I agree." He began to pick up the pieces.

The woodcutter spat out the stone. "But you could win easily."

The old man finally noticed him. "Are you still here?"

The woodcutter thought that this was his chance now to do a good deed. "It's been a most interesting game. However, if you—"

But the old man made shooing motions with his hands. "You should've gone home long ago."

"But I—" began the woodcutter.

The fat man rose. "Go home. It may already be too late."

That's a funny thing to say, the woodcutter thought. He turned around to get his things. But big, fat mushrooms had sprouted among the roots of the trees. A brown carpet surrounded him. He brushed the mushrooms aside until he found a rusty hatchet blade. He couldn't find a trace of the hatchet shaft or of his carrying pole.

Puzzled, he picked up the hatchet blade. "This can't be mine. My hatchet was practically new. Have you two gentlemen seen it?" He turned around again, but the two men had disappeared along with the chessboard and chess pieces.

"That's gratitude for you." Picking up the rusty hatchet blade, the woodcutter tried to make his way back through the woods; but he could not find the way he had come up. "It's like someone rearranged all the trees."

Somehow he made his way out of the mountains. However, fields and villages now stood where there had once been wooded hills. "What are you doing here?" he asked a farmer.

"What are you?" the farmer snorted, and went back to working in his field.

The woodcutter thought about telling him that he was swinging his hoe wrong, but he remembered what the two men had said. So he hurried home instead.

The woodcutter followed the river until he reached his own village, but as he walked through the fields, he didn't recognize one person. There was even a pond before the village gates. It had never been there before. He broke into a run, but there was a different house in the spot where his home had been. Even so, he burst into the place.

Two strange children looked up from the table, and a strange woman picked up a broom. "Out!"

The woodcutter raised his arms protectively. "Wait, I live here."

But the woman beat the woodcutter with a broom until he retreated into the street. By now, a crowd had gathered. The woodcutter looked around desperately. "What's happened to my village? Doesn't anyone know me?"

The village schoolteacher had come out of the school. He asked the woodcutter his name, and when the woodcutter told him, the schoolteacher pulled at his whiskers. "That name sounds familiar, but it can't be."

With the crowd following them, he led the woodcutter to the clan temple. "I collect odd, interesting stories." The schoolteacher got out a thick book. "There's a strange incident in the clan book." He leafed through the book toward the beginning and pointed to a name. "A woodcutter left the village and never came back." He added quietly. "But that was several thousand years ago."

"That's impossible," the woodcutter insisted. "I just stayed away to watch two men play a game of chess."

The schoolteacher sighed. "The two men must have been saints. Time doesn't pass for them as it does for us."

And at that moment, the woodcutter remembered his wife's warning.

But it was too late now.

SOURCE

NATIONAL
STORYTELLING
FESTIVAL

Jonesborough, Tennessee

Article

The Art of

Most traditional stories were passed along orally for generations before anyone wrote them down. Today, modern storytellers from diverse cultures continue the oral tradition. They share traditional tales and personal stories with audiences around the globe.

The National Storytelling Association, headquartered in Jonesborough, Tennessee, is dedicated to preserving and expanding the art of storytelling. Each year, the NSA holds a National Storytelling Festival. Some of the most renowned storytellers in the world perform there. You will meet some of them on these pages.

Storyteller	Childhood Home
 **DEREK BURROWS**	Burrows was born and raised in Nassau, Bahamas. He also spent a great deal of time on his grandparents' farm on Long Island, Bahamas.
 **DONALD DAVIS**	Davis grew up in the mountains of North Carolina, in an area settled by the Scottish. His rural community had no radios, electricity, or other modern conveniences until the 1950s.
 **OLGA LOYA**	Loya grew up in a Mexican-American neighborhood in Los Angeles, California, where her neighbors spoke a lively mixture of English and Spanish.

Storytelling

Why he/she became a storyteller	Origin of his/her stories	Special Techniques
While studying music, Burrows played with a group that performed ballads based on old European stories. Learning all those old stories made him think back to the stories he had heard as a child. He began to research the stories he remembered and to collect new tales from Bahamian friends. Today, Burrows uses stories and music to share his rich cultural heritage with others.	Burrows' stories come from the Caribbean. They contain elements of African stories, as well as elements of stories told by the Arawak—the first people to live on the Bahama Islands. Many of the stories are about traditional characters called B'Anase and B'Boukee.	Burrows likes to have his audience participate in his stories. He sometimes asks the audience to add phrases to a story or to respond to "Boonday," a traditional Bahamian storyteller's chant. Burrows often includes music in his performances, playing one or more of the fifteen instruments he has learned. He sometimes teaches the audience to sing parts of the songs he plays.
Wherever he went, new acquaintances asked Davis many questions about his rather unusual childhood. He found that the best way to answer them was by sharing childhood stories. When he returned home for visits, Davis collected additional stories from friends and neighbors.	Many of Davis's stories are traditional Appalachian stories called Jack Tales, which are based on ancient Scottish tales. Davis has also crafted a number of stories based on events from his own childhood.	Davis believes that stories are made of pictures. When he tells a story, he is trying to help the audience understand the pictures inside his head. Therefore, he uses lots of body language and descriptive language to tell his stories. Davis tailors his words and gestures to the audience at hand.
During Loya's childhood, storytelling was a part of everyday life. While working as a community organizer, Loya decided to plan a storytelling festival as a fundraiser for her community. She found herself not only organizing but performing as well.	Loya uses people and books as sources for traditional stories from all over the world. She also enjoys studying history and uses storytelling to share important stories from the past.	Loya uses sound effects to add humor or suspense to a tale. She likes to use some Spanish when she tells stories to an English-speaking audience, so that listeners can appreciate the music of the language. Using Spanish also helps Loya convey the authentic voices of traditional Hispanic story characters, such as Coyote and Tía Miseria.

How to Tell a Story

Storytellers use gestures and different expressions to help tell a story.

Storytellers' gestures are often written into their story script.

Storytelling is a tradition that began in ancient cultures. Early storytellers passed their tales down orally from generation to generation. Many of those stories still exist today.

What is a storyteller? A storyteller is someone who can tell stories in ways that make them come alive. Some storytellers change the sound of their voices, wear costumes, use props, sing, or speak in rhyme as they tell their stories.

Music or sound effects can help set a mood or feeling for a story.

from
"How the Coyote Gets His Name"
by Jerry Tello

...so all the animals gathered their young and took them back to where they slept and as the coyote was walking up (walking motion) the hill, he was thinking, "How can I be first...how can I be first??!!" (Make pensive face—look at extended finger.)

By this time, the Sun (look up) had finished his cycle and touched (tap-on-the-shoulder motion with index finger) the Moon on the shoulder and Ms. Moon began sharing her brilliance.

And there sat (sitting action) the coyote on top of the hill, under a tree, still thinking how he could be first (index finger to temple, as if thinking), when he had a brilliant idea!

(Eyes wide, mouth open). "I'll just stay up all night!" That way, I'll see Mr. Sun as he awakes and I can be first!"

Well, several hours passed and as hard as the coyote tried, he was still getting tired (eyes drooping). In his struggle to keep awake, he glanced up (look up) at the tree branches and had a good idea and thought to himself, "I'll just break two small branches and put one in each eyelid to keep me awake!"

So the coyote did just that (motion of reaching up, breaking branches)... except that in a short time, the coyote was fast asleep with his eyes wide open (index finger and thumb of each hand, holding eyes wide open.)

The moon finished her cycle and several hours later, the coyote finally awoke and ran to the circle (running motion), where he saw no one except the big brown animal standing on the rock. Thinking he was first, the coyote said (stand up straight), "OK, I'm ready to pick and I want to be the Bear so I can stand on the rock and make all the announcements!"

1 Write Your Script

Choose a story that you would like to tell others. It could be a well-known fairy tale, a myth, or an experience from your own life. Create a script to help you learn your story. Organize it in a way that is useful to you. Some storytellers like to work from an outline that lists the major events of the story, then fill in the details orally. Others like to write down the whole story, using their own words. Write your first draft. Try to keep it short— about one or two pages.

TOOLS

- paper and pencil
- story to tell
- props and music (optional)

2 Plan Your Delivery

Look over your script. Think about the effect you want the story to have on your audience. Is your story happy or sad, funny or scary? You will want to create the right mood for your audience. Traditionally, storytellers have used many different methods to bring their stories to life. They make gestures, use props, change their voices, and use sound effects. Revise the first draft of your script by adding directions for yourself in the appropriate places. When you tell your story, you'll know just when to include special effects.

3 Practice Your Story

Practice telling your story. Refer to your script at first to make sure that you get the story right and that you know exactly when the gestures, props, music, or sound effects come into the story. Practice telling your story in front of a mirror so you can watch your movements. Tell it to a friend or a member of your family. Eventually you'll be able to tell the story from memory using all the special effects and props you've planned.

Tip Tape-record your special effects. Ask a helper to play the tape for you. Provide him or her with a marked script that shows when the tape should be played.

4 Tell Your Story

When you're happy with the way you tell the story, you will want to present it to an audience. Make arrangements to tell it to your classmates, a group of neighbors, or some of your friends. If your story is suitable for younger children, you might perform it for the kindergarteners or the first and second graders in your school. Be sure to assemble any props or costumes you will need.

If You Are Using a Computer ...

Use the Record and Playback tools to practice your story as you write it. Edit your story as you listen to how it sounds.

THINK

In what other situations might you use the storytelling skills you have learned?

José García
Drama Coach ▶

49

Through the performing arts, we entertain others.

On Stage

Find out what happens to Manuel when he enters the school talent show. Then read a poem about a school play.

Meet Doug Funnie, who doesn't appreciate his sister's talent.

Learn how drama coach José García inspires creativity in his students.

WORKSHOP 2

Write a dialogue for characters of your own creation.

VANESSA'S BAD GRADE
by Ross Brown
Scene Five
Vanessa is in her room when Theo walks in.
VANESSA: I got my history test back.
(She hands him the test paper.)
THEO: Whoa. This is a "D."
VANESSA: I know. I've never gotten a "D" before. I've seen them, but never next to my name.
THEO: And this one is in red. That's the worst kind to get.
VANESSA: I don't know how it happened. Robert and I studied for this.
THEO: Yeah, I saw that.

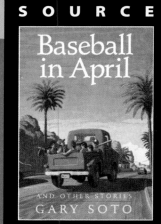
FROM **BASEBALL IN APRIL
AND OTHER STORIES
BY GARY SOTO**

LA BAMBA

Manuel was the fourth of seven children and looked like a lot of kids in his neighborhood: black hair, brown face, and skinny legs scuffed from summer play. But summer was giving way to fall: the trees were turning red, the lawns brown, and the pomegranate trees were heavy with fruit. Manuel walked to school in the frosty morning, kicking leaves and thinking of tomorrow's talent show. He was still amazed that he had volunteered. He was going to pretend to sing Ritchie Valens's "La Bamba" before the entire school.

Why did I raise my hand? he asked

ILLUSTRATED BY JOSÉ ORTEGA

himself, but in his heart he knew the answer. He yearned for the limelight. He wanted applause as loud as a thunderstorm, and to hear his friends say, "Man, that was bad!" And he wanted to impress the girls, especially Petra Lopez, the second-prettiest girl in his class. The prettiest was already taken by his friend Ernie. Manuel knew he should be reasonable, since he himself was not great-looking, just average.

Manuel kicked through the fresh-fallen leaves. When he got to school he realized he had forgotten his math workbook. If the teacher found out, he would have to stay after school and miss practice for the talent show. But fortunately for him, they did drills that morning.

During lunch Manuel hung around with Benny, who was also in the talent show. Benny was going to play the trumpet in spite of the fat lip he had gotten playing football.

"How do I look?" Manuel asked. He cleared his throat and started moving his lips in pantomime. No words came out, just a hiss that sounded like a snake. Manuel tried to look emotional, flailing his arms on the high notes and opening his eyes and mouth as wide as he could when he came to "*Para bailar la baaaaammmba.*"

After Manuel finished, Benny said it looked all right, but suggested Manuel dance while he sang. Manuel thought for a moment and decided it was a good idea.

"Yeah, just think you're like Michael Jackson or someone like that," Benny suggested. "But don't get carried away."

During rehearsal, Mr. Roybal, nervous about his debut as the school's talent coordinator, cursed under his breath when the lever that controlled the speed on the record player jammed.

"Darn," he growled, trying to force the lever. "What's wrong with you?"

"Is it broken?" Manuel asked, bending over for a closer look. It looked all right to him.

Mr. Roybal assured Manuel that he would have a good record player at the talent show, even if it meant bringing his own stereo from home.

Manuel sat in a folding chair, twirling his record on his thumb. He watched a skit about personal hygiene, a mother-and-daughter

violin duo, five first-grade girls jumping rope, a karate kid breaking boards, three girls singing, and a skit about the pilgrims. If the record player hadn't been broken, he would have gone after the karate kid, an easy act to follow, he told himself.

As he twirled his forty-five record, Manuel thought they had a great talent show. The entire school would be amazed. His mother and father would be proud, and his brothers and sisters would be jealous and pout. It would be a night to remember.

Benny walked onto the stage, raised his trumpet to his mouth, and waited for his cue. Mr. Roybal raised his hand like a symphony conductor and let it fall dramatically. Benny inhaled and blew so loud that Manuel dropped his record, which rolled across the cafeteria floor until it hit a wall. Manuel raced after it, picked it up, and wiped it clean.

"Boy, I'm glad it didn't break," he said with a sigh.

That night Manuel had to do the dishes and a lot of homework, so he could only practice in the shower. In bed he prayed that he wouldn't mess up. He prayed that it wouldn't be like when he was a first-grader. For Science Week he had wired together a C battery and a bulb, and told everyone he had discovered how a flashlight worked. He was so pleased with himself that he practiced for hours pressing the wire to the battery, making the bulb wink a dim, orangish light. He showed it to so many kids in his neighborhood that when it was time to show his class how a flashlight worked, the battery was dead. He pressed the wire to the battery, but the bulb didn't respond. He pressed until his thumb hurt and some kids in the back started snickering.

But Manuel fell asleep confident that nothing would go wrong this time.

The next morning his father and mother beamed at him. They were proud that he was going to be in the talent show.

"I wish you would tell us what you're doing," his mother said. His father, a pharmacist who wore a blue smock with his name on a plastic rectangle, looked up from the newspaper and sided with his wife. "Yes, what are you doing in the talent show?"

"You'll see," Manuel said with his mouth full of Cheerios.

The day whizzed by, and so did his afternoon chores and dinner.

Suddenly he was dressed in his best clothes and standing next to Benny backstage, listening to the commotion as the cafeteria filled with school kids and parents. The lights dimmed, and Mr. Roybal, sweaty in a tight suit and a necktie with a large knot, wet his lips and parted the stage curtains.

"Good evening, everyone," the kids behind the curtain heard him say. "Good evening to you," some of the smart-alecky kids said back to him.

"Tonight we bring you the best John Burroughs Elementary has to offer, and I'm sure that you'll be both pleased and amazed that our little school houses so much talent. And now, without further ado, let's get on with the show." He turned and, with a swish of his hand, commanded, "Part the curtain." The curtains parted in jerks. A girl dressed as a toothbrush and a boy dressed as a dirty gray tooth walked onto the stage and sang:

Brush, brush, brush
Floss, floss, floss
Gargle the germs away—
hey! hey! hey!

After they finished singing, they turned to Mr. Roybal, who dropped his hand. The toothbrush dashed around the stage after the dirty tooth, which was laughing and having a great time until it slipped and nearly rolled off the stage.

Mr. Roybal jumped out and caught it just in time. "Are you OK?"

The dirty tooth answered, "Ask my dentist," which drew laughter and applause from the audience.

The violin duo played next, and except for one time when the girl got lost, they sounded fine. People applauded, and some even stood up. Then the first-grade girls maneuvered onto the stage while jumping rope. They were all smiles and bouncing ponytails as a hundred cameras flashed at once. Mothers "awhed" and fathers sat up proudly.

The karate kid was next. He did a few kicks, yells, and chops, and finally, when his father held up a board, punched it in two. The audience clapped and looked at each other, wide-eyed with respect. The boy bowed to the audience, and father and son ran off the stage.

Manuel remained behind the stage shivering with fear. He mouthed the words to "La Bamba" and swayed from left to right. Why did he raise his hand and volunteer? Why couldn't he

more sweaty than before, took Manuel's forty-five record and placed it on a new record player.

"You ready?" Mr. Roybal asked.

"Yeah…"

Mr. Roybal walked back on stage and announced that Manuel Gomez, a fifth-grader in Mrs. Knight's class, was going to pantomime Richie Valens's classic hit "La Bamba."

The cafeteria roared with applause. Manuel was nervous but loved the noisy crowd. He pictured his mother and father applauding loudly and his brothers and sisters also clapping, though not as energetically.

Manuel walked on stage and the song started immediately. Glassy-eyed from the shock of being in front of so many people, Manuel moved his lips and swayed in a made-up dance step. He couldn't see his parents, but he could see his brother Mario, who was a year younger, thumb-wrestling with a friend. Mario was wearing Manuel's favorite shirt; he would deal with Mario later. He saw some other kids get up and head for the drinking fountain, and a baby sitting in the middle of an aisle sucking her thumb and watching him intently.

have just sat there like the rest of the kids and not said anything? While the karate kid was on stage, Mr. Roybal,

What am I doing here? thought Manuel. This is no fun at all. Everyone was just sitting there. Some people were moving to the beat, but most were just watching him, like they would a monkey at the zoo.

But when Manuel did a fancy dance step, there was a burst of applause and some girls screamed. Manuel tried another dance step. He heard more applause and screams and started getting into the groove as he shivered and snaked like Michael Jackson around the stage. But the record got stuck, and he had to sing

Para bailar la bamba
Para bailar la bamba
Para bailar la bamba
Para bailar la bamba

again and again.

Manuel couldn't believe his bad luck. The audience began to laugh and stand up in their chairs. Manuel remembered how the forty-five record had dropped from his hand and rolled across the cafeteria floor. It probably got scratched, he thought, and now it was stuck, and he was stuck dancing and moving his lips to the same words over and over. He had never been so embarrassed. He would have to ask his parents to move the family out of town.

After Mr. Roybal ripped the needle across the record, Manuel slowed his dance steps to a halt. He didn't know what to do except bow to the audience, which applauded wildly, and scoot off the stage, on the verge of tears. This was worse than the homemade flashlight. At least no one laughed then, they just snickered.

Manuel stood alone, trying hard to hold back the tears as Benny, center stage, played his trumpet. Manuel was jealous because he sounded great, then mad as he recalled that it was Benny's loud trumpet playing that made the forty-five record fly out of his hands. But when the entire cast lined up for a curtain call, Manuel received a burst of applause that was so loud it shook the walls of the cafeteria. Later, as he mingled with the kids and parents, everyone patted him on the shoulder and told him, "Way to go. You were really funny."

Funny? Manuel thought. Did he do something funny?

Funny. Crazy. Hilarious. These were the words people said to him. He was confused, but beyond caring. All he knew was that people were paying attention to him, and his brother and sisters looked at him with a mixture of

jealousy and awe. He was going to pull Mario aside and punch him in the arm for wearing his shirt, but he cooled it. He was enjoying the limelight. A teacher brought him cookies and punch, and the popular kids who had never before given him the time of day now clustered around him. Ricardo, the editor of the school bulletin, asked him how he made the needle stick.

"It just happened," Manuel said, crunching on a star-shaped cookie.

At home that night his father, eager to undo the buttons on his shirt and ease into his La-Z-Boy recliner, asked Manuel the same thing, how he managed to make the song stick on the words "*Para bailar la bamba.*"

Manuel thought quickly and reached for scientific jargon he had read in magazines. "Easy, Dad. I used laser tracking with high optics and low functional decibels per channel." His proud but confused father told him to be quiet and go to bed.

"Ah, *que niños tan truchas,*" he said as he walked to the kitchen for a glass of milk. "I don't know how you kids nowadays get so smart."

Manuel, feeling happy, went to his bedroom, undressed, and slipped into his pajamas. He looked in the mirror and began to pantomime "La Bamba," but stopped because he was tired of the song. He crawled into bed. The sheets were as cold as the moon that stood over the peach tree in their backyard.

He was relieved that the day was over. Next year, when they asked for volunteers for the talent show, he wouldn't raise his hand. Probably.

School

from REMEMBERING AND
OTHER POEMS

BY MYRA COHN LIVINGSTON
ILLUSTRATED BY CURTIS PARKER

Play

I played the princess.
I had to stay
inside a barrel.
The prince hid away
in a keg right beside me.
Our hearts nearly sank
when the Pirate King said
we would both walk the plank.
Then our captain appeared
and he offered them gold
as a ransom, and that's when
the Pirate King told
us to come out
and plead our case,
and I climbed out and
slipped
and fell flat
on my face.

But it wasn't so bad
in the ending
because
all the audience gave us
a lot of
applause.

DouG
CAN'T DIG IT

based on a series created by Jim Jinkins
TV script by Ken Scarborough

Doug just knows his theatrical older sister Judy will do something to embarrass him at the school assembly. Worst of all, he's supposed to announce her performance! Will he step into the spotlight—or hide behind the curtains?

WIRED WORDS

Reading a TV script is different than reading a book or play. As you read, imagine that you are a director "seeing" this script come to life. Look for these directing terms as you read along:

CU: Close Up

DISSOLVE TO: The scene will fade out and change to a new scene.

INT: Interior. This refers to a specific location, like the inside of a room or building.

O.S: Off stage. A character talks from outside the scene in the picture.

SFX: Sound Effects

V.O: Voice Over. A character narrates a scene without appearing on camera.

MEET THE CAST

DOUG FUNNIE

Like any normal 11-and-a-half-year-old, Doug's main goal is to make it to junior high in one piece. Doug's daydreams help him get through sticky situations.

Porkchop
Doug's humanlike dog is his best animal friend, and Doug's advisor in times of trouble.

Judy Funnie
Doug's older sister has a different goal — to be the most famous actress of all time. Performing is her life!

Skeeter
Doug's best friend is a pretty cool customer. He thinks Doug gets too worked up about things sometimes.

Roger
Smart-mouthed Roger's favorite hobby is giving Doug a hard time.

Mrs. Wingo
Doug's teacher has every confidence in Judy's talent. If only Doug did, too.

Mr. Bone
Bluffington Elementary's Vice Principal will make sure that Doug is at that assembly.

Doug and its characters are created by Jim Jinkins.

Fade in: Int. Doug's Room—Night. Doug sits at his desk, writing.

Doug

Dear Journal: me again. Doug. Sorry I didn't write yesterday—I was too busy having a heart attack. It all started...

Int. Kitchen—Morning. Doug and Porkchop having breakfast.

Doug (V.O.)

...yesterday morning.

SFX: Loud Opera Music (Carmen—"Toreador Song")
Suddenly, Judy bursts in, wearing matador regalia and swinging a stick like a sword. She stalks Doug.

Judy

(sings)
"Toreador, en ga-a-a-rde!"
Take that!

Doug

Hey! Mom, Judy's doing that bullfighter thing again.

Judy plops down opposite Doug and stares at him.

Judy

I know something you don-hon't.

Doug

What?

Judy

"Toreador..."

She grins at him, and then, suddenly, springs up and leaves, singing.

Doug

(to Porkchop)
You know, Porkchop, sometimes I'm really glad Judy goes to her own school instead of ours.

Doug (V.O.)
Then, in class, Mrs. Wingo made the announcement...

Dissolve to: Int. Classroom—Day. Mrs. Wingo stands in front of the class.

Mrs. Wingo
Tomorrow afternoon, there will be a special school assembly, and it's going to be introduced by Doug.

Doug smiles to himself.

Dissolve to: Fantasy. A spotlight appears on a deep red curtain. Doug pops through the curtain, dressed in a snappy tuxedo. He steps up to the microphone.

Doug
Good afternoon, everybody. I'm really happy to be here. Of course I'm really happy to be anywhere except class.

SFX: Rimshot, Enormous Laughter

Doug
But seriously—

Mrs. Wingo (O.S.)
Doug?

Dissolve to: Back to reality. Angle on Mrs. Wingo.

Mrs. Wingo
Doug? Don't you want to know who you're introducing? She asked for you especially.

Doug
Who?

Mrs. Wingo
Your sister. Judy. She's going to perform for all of us.

CU Doug. Pure terror—perhaps the picture rotates a little, with a weirdly distorted classroom around him.

Doug
Judy?

Dissolve to: Fantasy. Int. Auditorium Stage
Judy is dressed like a beatnik. There are large projections of her every place. She bangs the bongoes in counterpoint to her words.

Judy
My *soul* throbs!
I am...your washing machine!

(brightly)
Red towel!

(sinister hush)
Pink underwear.

(loud)
Buzzzz! Unbalanced load!

Suddenly she leaps up! She caws like a chicken and flaps her wings.

Angle on the audience. Doug is in the middle, reddening in embarrassment.

Angle on Judy. She clutches her brow and bows her head as the lights flick to a single spotlight from above.

Judy
Doug loves Patti.

A gigantic backdrop drops in behind her, showing Doug and Patti in a big heart.

Angle on Doug. The audience around him is laughing hideously. We zoom in on Doug's face, frozen in fear.

Dissolve to: Int. Honker Burger. Doug and Skeeter are sitting across from each other in the same booth. They are both slumped over shakes.

Skeeter
Maybe it won't be so bad, Doug. Maybe it'll be neat.

Doug glares at Skeeter.

Skeeter

I mean...awful. Did I say neat? Terrible, I meant.

Suddenly Judy and about three of her friends burst in the front door of the restaurant, and barge up to the counter.

Friend #1

(sings)

Give us shakes, chocolate and ta-a-sty. With some fries, but don't be ha-a-sty.

Judy

Catsup, mustard, mayo, lettuce, just make sure you don't forget us!

Angle on Doug and Skeeter.

Skeeter

I think I see what you mean.

Roger (O.S.)

Hey, Funnie!

Doug looks over to where Roger, Willy, Ned and Boomer are sitting.

Roger

This is a preview of tomorrow's show? I can't wait to see it!

They all laugh.

CU Doug. Trying to smile along, he looks toward another table. Judy and her friends are just sitting down. Judy steps up into the booth, puts one foot on the table, holding aloft a milkshake.

Judy

Alas, poor Strawberry!

Her friends applaud.

Angle on Doug and Skeeter.

Doug

I have to stop her. For her own sake.

Skeeter

How can you do that?

Doug

Maybe if I get on her good side. Maybe if...I use a little psychology.

Angle on Judy's booth. Doug approaches.

Doug

Hey, Judy—

Judy turns coolly/calmly to Doug.

Judy

Yes-I'm-performing-at-your-school-tomorrow-and-no-there's-nothing-you-can-do-to-change-my-mind.

Doug

Oh, okay, see you later.

Angle on Skeeter's table. Doug slumps back.

Skeeter

Did you use psychology on her, Doug?

Doug

This is going to be harder than I thought.

Skeeter

I think I have an idea.

Skeeter stands up and whispers in Doug's ear.
Int. Judy's room—Day. CU Judy.

Judy

I hate you! I hate you! I hate hate *hate...*

SFX: Phone ringing. Judy immediately drops her character
and picks up the phone.

Judy

(sweetly)
Hel*lo?*

Voice

Hello, is this Judy Funnie the actress?

Judy

Yes, it is. Who is this please?

Voice

Oh, you don't know me, but I'm a very famous producer.

Cut to: Int. Den—Day. Doug is talking into the handkerchief-
covered phone. Skeeter is crouched across the desk from him.

Skeeter

J.B. Hunkamunca.

Doug

J.B. Hunkamunca.

Doug covers the mouthpiece.

Doug

(hisses)

She'll never buy that! (into phone) You what? You say you've *heard of
me?* Well, I called to tell you you shouldn't do that show tomorrow.

Judy (O.S.)

Really?

Skeeter looks up. His mouth drops open. He starts trying to signal Doug.

Wider Angle revealing Judy, who's just come in the door.

Doug

It's not right for you...I feel like it's the wrong...well, just don't do it!

Judy moves from the door to the desk.

Judy

Really, Mr. Hunkamunca? Well, I suppose I'll just have to cancel it, then.

Skeeter starts poking Doug and pointing to Judy. Doug brushes him away, and Skeeter, in despair, buries his head in his hands.

Doug

Really? Great! Well, goodbye!

Doug hangs up.

Doug
She bought it, Skeet!
(bewildered)
...*Skeet?*

Doug turns to Judy.

Doug
What'samatter with Skeeter?

Judy
I haven't the faintest.

Doug
You haven't the—
(getting it)
Uh-oh.

Judy
Doug, why can't you dig it?

Doug
Huh?

Judy
You know, this is exactly why you need me to perform at your school.

She stomps to the door, throws it open and makes a theatrical exit.

Judy
Tomorrow you'll thank me, Mr. Hunkamunca.

She goes, slamming the door. Doug sighs and turns to Skeeter.

Doug
No—tomorrow I'm going to have a heart attack. Judy's never performed anything that made me want to thank her. I'll never forget the last time we were on stage together. It was a disaster.

Dissolve to: Flashback. Int. Auditorium—Day. The set is the inside of a mouth. A bunch of kids are dressed as teeth. Judy is dressed as plaque, and is attacking them.

Doug (V.O.)
It was the Dental Hygiene play. I was the toothbrush—Judy was plaque.

Judy
Here are the teeth that wouldn't brush. Now I will come and turn them to mush!

All Teeth
Help! Help, save us Mr. Toothbrush!

Doug enters, dressed as a toothbrush complete with superhero cape. He brushes Judy.

Doug
Here I am and plaque I will crush! Take that and that!

Judy begins to die elaborately.

Doug
And now all plaque is gone.

Judy
Uhhhhhh....

Doug notices Judy is still staggering around.

Doug
(louder)
And now plaque is gone!

Judy
Uhhhhh....

SFX: Audience snickers

Doug
Judy!

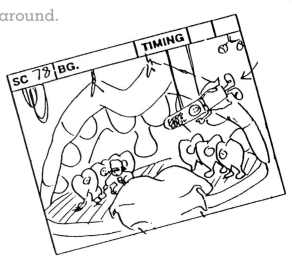

Doug reddens in embarrassment. He goes over and tries to brush her off stage. Flats fall down, Teeth run everywhere. General hub-bub.

SFX: Audience laughs

CU Doug, reddening in extreme embarrassment.

Doug
Yup, that play just about killed me.

Cut to: Int. School Hallway. The class moves along the hallway toward the door to the auditorium.

Doug (V.O.)
So there I was faced with another of Judy's performances, only problem was, I couldn't think of one good reason to get me out of it.

Roger comes up next to Doug.

Roger
Hey, Funnie! I can't believe it! You're really gonna go through with it?

The class files into the auditorium door. Roger pushes in in front of Doug.

Roger
Well, Funnie, I hope you and your goofy sister have fun—it's your funeral! Ha ha ha.

Doug hesitates. He looks around and keeps walking down the corridor. Porkchop follows. Doug, looking behind him, comes into this corridor and closes the door behind Porkchop.

Doug (V.O.)
I just needed a minute to think.

Cut to: Int. Auditorium Stage. Lamarr Bone confronts Mrs. Wingo behind the curtain.

Bone

Where's Funnie? We got a show to do!

Cut to: Int. Corridor. Doug is still pacing. He stops and looks at Porkchop.

Doug

What do you think, Porkchop? Should I go in front of everyone and introduce Judy?

Porkchop

(whines)

Doug

You're right. It could be the Dental Hygiene Play all over again.

Doug stops pacing in front of the door he came in through— the one that goes back out to the hallway. He considers it. Then Doug turns away from the door.

Doug

Boy, sure could use a little fresh air, Porkchop. How about you?

Another angle. Doug is at the other end of the corridor and is confronted with three unmarked doors. He hesitates, then chooses one and goes through it.

Doug

This way, I think.

Cut to: Int. Stage

Angle on Doug. It is very dark. Doug blinks. He reacts with surprise.

Doug (V.O.)

And there she was.

Judy, in beatnik garb, nervously peeks through the curtains at the audience. Mrs. Wingo stands next to her.

Judy

This could be a very important performance for me. Shakespeare did his first performance for his brother's grade school. Did you know that?

Angle on Doug. He turns to the curtain next to him and peeks out. Roger and some of his friends are laughing.

Angle on Judy and Bone

Bone

Well, can't find him. Let's get this show on the road.
(shouts offscreen)
Dim the lights!

Judy

But you told Doug I wanted him to introduce me, right?

SFX: Kids cheer

Angle on Doug, nervously looking from Judy to the door next to him labelled "Exit."

Mrs. Wingo (O.S.)

Now, dear, we have to start.

Judy

But, we have to wait for Doug. I—I wanted him to see this.

Bone

Now listen, young lady...

Doug

Wait! I'm here.

Dissolve to: Int. Auditorium. Doug is at the microphone, quieting the applause.

SFX: Applause, Whistles

Doug

Hello, everyone, I'm Doug Funnie and here's someone I've known all of my life and most of hers, my sister, performance artist Judy Funnie.

SFX: Applause, Hoots, Whistles

Cut to: Int. Hallway Outside of Auditorium—Day.

Doug paces nervously.

Doug (V.O.)
So in the end I stood up for Judy's act. But that didn't mean I wanted to sit down and actually watch it.

He hears something and stops pacing.

Doug (V.O.)
But then I heard something I never expected.

SFX: Muffled laughter, then scattered light applause

Doug, curious, creeps over to the auditorium door and opens it a crack. He sees a few people clapping. As Doug turns away from the door in some confusion to consider this, suddenly, BLAM! The door flies open and kids pour out, knocking Doug left and right in their hurry. All around him he hears the comments of his schoolmates.

Kids

—Wow! It was great!

—I didn't get it.

—I hated it, but I liked her hair.

—Very symbolic.

A hand comes in and pulls Doug out of the crowd. Doug finds himself face-to-face with Roger.

Roger

Hey, Funnie, you want to know what I thought of that show?

Doug

Well...

Roger

I *loved* it! It was *great*.

Doug

Really?

Roger throws his arm around Doug.

Roger

Yeah. It completely got me out of having to take a math test! Ha ha ha. Tell your sister she can come back anytime she likes.

Doug looks at Roger in amazement.

Dissolve to: Int. Auditorium—Later. Doug walks through the door at the back of the deserted auditorium. There is a group gathered around Judy on the stage. Doug walks up and stands by the sidelines.

Photographer

Can we get a picture for the Daily Honk, Judy?

Judy

Sure, just a second.

She breaks away from the group and goes over to Doug.

Judy

(quietly)

Come on, Doug.

Doug

Awww....

Wider angle. Judy drags a showily reluctant Doug to center stage. They pose. With a flash they freeze; the colors bleed out until it's black and white.

Doug (V.O.)

So I guess it turned out all right.

Angle on Judy and Doug

Dissolve to: Int. Doug's Room—Night. We Pull Out from the picture, which is tacked to the bulletin board behind Doug's head. Doug is writing in his diary.

SFX: Opera music from other room

Doug (V.O.)

I didn't need to have a heart attack after all. Not only was it not embarrassing, but I think Judy's actually quite...good. No: quite... sisterly. No: quite...

Suddenly the door bursts open. The music and Judy (dressed as a toreador) and Porkchop (dressed as a bull) all blast in, taking over Doug's room.

Doug

...embarrassing. She's quite embarrassing.

Ext. House—Night.

Doug (V.O.)

Juuuudyyyy!

Fade out.

José García

Drama Coach

This coach *teaches* kids how to *act up!*

When you watch a movie, TV show, or play, the actors' performances often seem perfect. How do actors learn the tricks of their trade? If they're lucky, they have the help of a good drama coach like José García. García works with professional actors. He also teaches young people about acting and helps them prepare to give school presentations.

PROFILE

Name: José García

Occupation: drama coach

Previous jobs: substitute teacher, actor, set designer, maskmaker

Favorite actors: James Caan and Geraldine Page

Favorite play: *The Blood Wedding* by Federico García Lorca

Favorite story as a fifth grader: *The Lord of the Rings* by J.R.R. Tolkien

Most embarrassing moment on stage: "While showing off during a high school singing concert, I pushed my voice so much that I went flat."

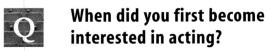QUESTIONS

for José García

Here's how **drama coach José García** *trains* performers to *exercise* their **creativity.**

Q **When did you first become interested in acting?**

A I created my own skits with friends as early as second grade. I even won the sixth-grade talent show at my school!

Q **Who attends your acting workshops?**

A I coach professional actors preparing for roles. I also work with kids who want to learn about acting, or who are preparing for school plays or other presentations.

Q **Do all actors need coaches?**

A Like any skill, acting is easier for some people than for others, but training is always important.

Q **Many of your students have no acting experience. How do you get them started?**

A I put them through a lot of exercises. I want them to be able to work with their whole bodies, from the tips of their toes to their hair follicles! Actors cannot work effectively unless their whole bodies are loose.

Q **What kinds of exercises do you do?**

A One favorite exercise involves masks. The students and I put on masks and move our faces and bodies silently. We try to convey the feeling of the masks through body language. As time goes on, we add sound, and eventually speech.

How do you help students prepare to perform in plays?

 We begin by reading through the script. We spend time analyzing the characters. Actors need to know their characters inside and out. Then they can begin to "play" with the roles and make them their own.

 What's the most important skill an actor can have?

 I'd have to say sincerity. You have to believe in the role you are playing. If you are sincere, you will win over your audience.

 Many people worry about stage fright. What is it?

Butterflies in the stomach, trembling, anxiety, and fear of failure. It can be scary, but without it you don't have the edge. It's that excitement that allows an artist to work on a heightened level.

 Besides working with actors, what things might you do in a typical day?

 I write plays and screenplays, and I spend time researching them. I also have to promote myself as an actor and drama coach. It takes a lot of work to get work! When I have time left over, I design masks and drama sets.

José García's
Tips for Young Performers

1 **Learn everything you can about your craft. There's always room to learn and improve.**

2 **Discover your own natural talents and strive to expand them. Don't try to be like someone else.**

3 **Don't allow others to discourage you. Believe in yourself.**

How to
Write a Dialogue

When a movie, play, or TV show is written, the writer must decide what the characters will say to each other. He writes down their words, or dialogue, in script form for the actors to learn.

What is a dialogue? A dialogue is a conversation between two or more characters or people. When you talk with a friend, your conversation is called a dialogue.

A dialogue script has a title. The author's name goes beneath the title.

A brief description sets the scene of the dialogue.

Character names are written in capital letters so that they will not be confused with the lines of dialogue.

Photo courtesy of NBC

● Stage directions are written in parentheses.

VANESSA'S BAD GRADE
by Ross Brown
Scene Five

Vanessa is in her room when Theo walks in.

VANESSA: I got my history test back. (She hands him the test paper.)

THEO: Whoa. This is a "D."

VANESSA: I know. I've never gotten a "D" before. I've seen them, but never next to my name.

THEO: And this one is in red. That's the worst kind to get.

VANESSA: I don't know how it happened. Robert and I studied for this.

THEO: Yeah, I saw that.

VANESSA: When do you think I should tell Mom and Dad?

THEO: The sooner the better.

VANESSA: But if I tell them now, they might not let me go to the dance with Robert.

THEO: Vanessa, there is a chance that you may never dance again.

VANESSA: But how can they get angry? I've been getting "A's" all along. This is one little "D."

THEO: When it comes to Mom and Dad, there are no little "D's."

Vanessa Huxtable

EXAM (D)

X

X

X

1 Create Your Characters

The first step in writing a dialogue is to create the characters who will do the talking. Knowing your characters will help you to decide what type of dialogue to write. For example, a conversation between a grandmother and her grandson will be different from an argument between two friends.

TOOLS

- Paper and a pencil
- Colored pencils

Write a short description of each character. Include physical characteristics (height, hair color, etc.), as well as personality traits. As you write the dialogue, your descriptions will remind you of what your characters are like. Later, they will help your readers to "get in character" for their roles.

2 Choose a Topic

Now that you have created characters, you need to decide what they will talk about. They could be doing something as simple as walking through their neighborhood, talking about what they see. Or perhaps they're at home, discussing something that happened to them earlier in the day. Write down a brief description of the topic to go with your character descriptions.

3 Write Your Dialogue

Review your character descriptions and topic of conversation. Decide how you want the conversation to begin. Start writing! Think about the way a real conversation begins and how it builds. Think about what each of your characters would say and how he or she would say it. Try to make your dialogue sound like a real conversation between real people. Write down the conversation. Each time a different character begins to speak, you should write his or her name followed by a colon. (Use the dialogue on page 85 as a guide.)

Tip Once you've written a dialogue, read it aloud. Does it sound natural—like a real conversation? If not, make some changes and read it aloud again.

4 Perform Your Dialogue

Invite some friends or classmates to play the characters in your dialogue. You may want to take on one of the roles yourself, or be the "director" and help your "actors" to get in character and read the parts as you had envisioned them. Read through the dialogue a few times. When you and your fellow actors are satisfied with the way it sounds, you might want to perform it for your class.

If You Are Using a Computer ...

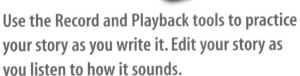

Use the Record and Playback tools to practice your story as you write it. Edit your story as you listen to how it sounds.

THINK
What did writing a dialogue show you about the way that we express ourselves through ordinary conversation?

José García
Drama Coach ▶

Speak Out

Meet Dinah Seabrooke,
who hopes to persuade
her classmates to vote
for her. Find out how to
give a great speech.

Read about the
Gettysburg
Address and
other famous
speeches.

Study famous
quotations on a
time line of historic
speeches in the
United States.

PROJECT

Prepare and deliver the stage
presentation of your choice.

from

DINAH for President

by Claudia Mills
illustrated by Michael Steirnagle

*Ever since Dinah Seabrooke entered the race for sixth grade president,
she's been trying to get across her campaign message—recycling. She's got to
convince the students of JFK Middle School how important it is to recycle the
school's trash.*

*The election is only a few days away, and Dinah has to think of some
creative ways to make her point. So far, she's made posters, and even worn
a recycling bucket on her head. How will she manage to top that?*

Benjamin was crawling. The Seabrookes spent most of Sunday
afternoon out in their backyard watching him inch his way forward
across an old quilt spread on the grass.

"Of course, it's not true crawling yet," Dinah's mother explained to
her. "With true crawling he'd be up on his hands and knees. This is what
you'd call creeping."

"But it counts," Dinah said. "For his baby book."

"You bet," her father said. He crouched down at the edge of the
quilt. "Come on, little guy! Come to Daddy."

With a big, drooly smile, Benjamin headed over to his father. He
propelled himself with his elbows, like an infant Marine dragging his
way across a patchwork jungle.

"Way to go, Benjamin!" His father grabbed him up for a tickling
hug, then set him down on the quilt again.

"Okay, Benjamin." Dinah took the next turn. "Come to me. Come to Dinah!" Sure enough, he crept in her direction.

Dinah was happy. For no reason at all, she was happy. Maybe it was the autumn sky, the newly washed blueness of it, bright and hard like the glaze on a porcelain bowl. The maple tree in the Harmons' yard was beginning to turn color, catching fire at the tips of the branches. The sun was warm, but the breeze had in it the sharp freshness of fall, Dinah's favorite season.

"I love the world," Dinah told Benjamin, flopping down on the quilt next to him. "Do you know how lucky you are to live here? In a world like this?"

"It'll do," her father said.

Flat on her back, Dinah gazed up at the sky. Maybe if more people lay on the grass and looked up, they wouldn't want to turn their world into a giant landfill. Or litter, or pollute. When Dinah was a famous actress she would use her fame to help environmental causes. She'd make television commercials for recycling, and people would say, "If a big movie star like Dinah Seabrooke believes in recycling, maybe we should, too." And if she were elected president of the United States someday, she'd make a law that everyone had to recycle, and she herself would use recycled paper for the invitations to her inaugural ball.

Dinah sat up. "The election is this coming Friday," she said. "That's just five days away. We'll have the debate in social studies on Wednesday, but only twenty-five people will be there to hear it. I have my two-minute speech at the assembly on Thursday, but two minutes isn't very long. I have to do something else, one more thing, so that every single sixth grader will know how much our school needs a recycling program."

"I suppose you could try wearing one of our trash cans on your head," Dinah's father suggested.

"Daddy! You're not being serious. I can't wear anything else on my head. It's against the dress code." All Dinah needed now was to be nicknamed Trash Can Head. Besides, wearing the bucket on her head hadn't really made the others understand anything about the importance of recycling. It had been a publicity stunt for Dinah herself, rather than a serious demonstration of the merits of her platform.

"I think you're doing enough," her mother said. "Your speech is sure to be wonderful, if I know my daughter."

That much was true. Dinah had already begun practicing her speech, and in her opinion it was every bit as good as Lincoln's Gettysburg Address. But the nagging doubts raised by Greg's poll refused to go away.

"No," she said. "I need one more thing."

Her parents exchanged glances.

"If you say so," her mother said. "But try not to get into any more trouble."

"I'll try," Dinah promised. But sometimes, despite her best intentions, trouble just *happened*.

On Monday morning, Dinah took the box of big plastic trash bags from the kitchen drawer and tucked it into her backpack. She had a plan. She'd stay after school and collect all the wastepaper thrown away that day, or as much of it as she could, and she'd carry it around with her throughout the day on Tuesday. Not on her head, just in a couple of trash bags she could drag behind her as she changed classes. *Look*, she'd say, *all of this was thrown away in one single day*. What more clear and dramatic way of showing the need for a schoolwide recycling program?

As soon as the 3:18 bell sounded, Dinah darted from room to room, eager to empty as many wastepaper baskets as she could in an hour. After half a dozen classrooms, her first trash bag was full almost to bursting. She left it next to her locker and started on another. In a few minutes, the second bag was full, as well.

On she raced down the long, silent halls of JFK Middle School, dumping basket after basket into her bags. The janitors would be surprised to find that some elf had arrived before them and spirited all the trash away.

By a quarter past four, Dinah was exhausted. She would never have guessed it was so much work to empty one school's trash baskets. Nor had she guessed one school could produce so much trash. Ten bulging sacks full of wastepaper stood in front of her locker.

Now what? Suddenly Dinah realized a fatal flaw in her plan. She couldn't fit even one trash bag into her narrow locker, let alone ten. There was no way she could haul all ten bags home with her on the crowded bus. But if she left them by her locker overnight, the janitors would cart them away.

"Curly Top!" Dinah turned to find Miss Brady staring down at her. "What on earth do you have in those bags?"

Pirate's treasure. Canned goods for the needy. Freshly washed gym wear. Dinah rapidly ran through a series of lies, then said in a voice that came out smaller and squeakier than she meant it to, "Trash."

"And what, may I ask, are you doing with ten bags of trash?"

Wearily, Dinah explained. How many points would Brady take off for unauthorized trash collection?

"Where do you think you're going to put them now that you've collected them?" Brady's voice kept jabbing at Dinah like a long, bony finger. "I don't suppose you thought of that, did you?"

"No," Dinah admitted. "I was thinking about it just now, when you found me."

"Well, how about the gym locker room?" Brady suggested crisply. "There's plenty of room there. I'll leave a note for the cleaning staff not to remove them. You can stop by and pick them up first thing in the morning."

Dinah's eyes widened. She opened her mouth and then shut it again.

"Well, don't stand there gaping like a goldfish," Miss Brady snapped at her. "Let's take them there before you miss the 4:30 bus."

Brady hoisted four of the bags, two in each hand, and strode down the hall with them. Dinah made herself follow with another two. Together they came back to collect the rest.

"You'd better go now," Brady told Dinah when all ten bags were lined up against the rear wall of the gym locker room. "Mind you, I want these out of here by the start of first period tomorrow, no ifs, ands, or buts."

"But—" Dinah had to know. "Why are you helping me?"

"You think you kids are the only ones who care about recycling?" Brady asked. "I think it's a crime what this school throws away. I've said so time and time again at faculty meetings."

"What happened?"

"Nothing. Maybe something will now. I doubt it, but it's worth a try. Okay, Curly Top, out of here."

"Thank you," Dinah managed to say.

Brady brushed it away with the back of her hand. "Go!" she boomed.

Dinah dashed for the bus.

The next morning Dinah ran to the gym locker room as soon as the school doors opened. Miss Brady helped her tie the bags together with the thick twine Dinah had brought from the utility room at home. Then, dragging the bags behind her like a mule pulling a barge down the Erie Canal, Dinah made her slow, laborious way to homeroom.

No one had noticed when Dinah caught her skirt in her locker door the first day. But everyone noticed someone pulling ten trash bags down the hall. They had to notice, or they'd trip and go sprawling.

"Hey, kid, get out of my way!" an eighth grader shouted at her. But he was the one who ended up getting out of the way.

Luckily Dinah had thought to hang a sign around her neck, so she didn't have to waste any precious breath on explanations.

THIS TRASH WAS COLLECTED

IN ONE DAY AT YOUR SCHOOL.

SHOULDN'T IT BE RECYCLED?

DINAH SEABROOKE SAYS YES!

DINAH SEABROOKE

FOR SIXTH-GRADE PRESIDENT!

"Dinah Seabrooke for sixth-grade janitor!" one boy jeered, but Dinah was too tired to respond. The hall stretched out before her endlessly. *Bumpity, bumpity, bumpity, bump.* She dragged her load up the long flight of middle-school stairs.

Another boy chanted, "Jason's in the White House, waiting to be elected. Dinah's in the garbage can, waiting to be collected!"

Very funny. On Dinah trudged, pulling the weight of the world behind her.

Homeroom at last. Dinah left her load just outside the door and sank into her seat.

"What do you have in those bags, Seabrooke?" Jason asked her. He paused, obviously trying to think of a hilarious answer to his own question. Then his face lit up. "Deodorant!" he said loudly. "Dinah just bought a week's supply of deodorant!"

"Oh, shut up," Blaine told him. Blaine? "At least Dinah cares about something. At least there's something she *believes* in."

"That's right, Dinah believes in deodorant!" Jason was laughing so hard he had trouble getting the last word out.

"You are so juvenile, I can't believe it," Blaine said. "Just ignore him, Dinah."

Dinah threw Blaine a grateful smile. These days she was certainly receiving assistance from unexpected quarters.

"No," Mr. Prensky said as Dinah began dragging her ten trash bags down the aisle to her seat. "No. I won't stand for it. No."

"No, what?" Dinah asked, but she knew.

"I will not permit you to disrupt this class another time with your ridiculous campaign, or whatever you call it."

"I'm just trying to save the planet," Dinah said coldly.

"Well, go save it in Mr. Roemer's office. Go. Now."

Dinah obeyed. She and her trash bags made their grand exit from first-period English.

"You again," Mr. Roemer said when the secretary ushered her into his office. "What is it this time?"

Dinah told him.

"I thought we had agreed that you weren't going to cause any more disturbances," Mr. Roemer said.

Dinah doubted that she had agreed to any such thing. When Dynamite Dinah was around, disturbances were only to be expected. And this time was different. How were people going to realize the enormity of the trash problem in their school if Dinah didn't make them actually *see* how much trash there was?

"I didn't wear anything on my head this time."

"I suppose we can be grateful for that," Mr. Roemer said. He studied the ten trash bags. "You really collected all that paper in one day?"

Dinah nodded. "This isn't even all of it."

"Well, if one of this year's class officers wants to take the initiative for a recycling program, I guess I'd look into it."

Dinah's heart soared. If Mr. Roemer looked into a recycling program, he'd have to see what a good idea it was. Now all she had to do was get herself elected president so that he'd look into it.

"All right, Dinah, go sit out by Mrs. MacDonald's desk for the rest of the period."

"What about my bags?"

"You'll have to leave them here."

"But I *need* them. People *should* be disturbed by them. I *want* them to be." Dinah's rush of joy was perilously close to becoming misery.

"Look," Mr. Roemer said, "suppose we leave them outside the main office, just for today, with your sign taped to the wall next to them. How would that be?"

"That would be wonderful." Dinah thought about hugging Mr. Roemer, but decided against it.

He walked to the door with her. "Remember, Dinah, the squeaky wheel may get the most grease, but it doesn't necessarily get the most votes."

But Mr. Roemer didn't understand. Dinah had to get the most votes. She just had to.

"Kids!" Mr. Dixon bellowed at the start of sixth period on Wednesday afternoon. "Clear your desks! Clear your minds! Today's the day we've been waiting for. Illustrious candidates, take your places."

Mr. Dixon set three chairs at the front of the room, facing the rows of desks. Dinah picked the chair farthest from Mr. Dixon.

She liked to go last when she had a presentation to make. The last speech had the greatest impact.

"Each candidate will give a two-minute speech, then each will get two minutes to respond to the speeches made by the others. After that we'll open the floor for questions. Winfield, you're on."

Jason stood up. He looked tan and athletic and sure of himself.

"Why should you elect me president of your class? Because I have a proven record of leadership in sports. I was captain of my youth-league baseball team last year, and it came in second in the whole city. Being a team captain taught me a lot about getting along with people and getting them to work together toward a common goal. I learned how to make hard decisions and how to stick by them afterward.

"Right now I'm on the football team, and I'm the only sixth grader who's gotten to play in a game so far this fall. I plan to go out for the basketball and baseball teams, too.

"My dad says that sports are like life, and life is like sports. Don't you want a *winner* to lead your class as president? If you elect me as president, I'll work hard all year to turn JFK into a school of champions."

Some of the boys began to cheer, but Dixon rapped on his desk with the pointer. "Hold your applause. You'll get your say at the polls on Friday. Yarborough."

Blaine took her place. She looked pale, but composed.

"The greatest problem our school faces today—" Blaine paused for emphasis "—is apathy. A lot of people in this school just don't care about their schoolwork, about extracurricular activities, about their *school*. Less than half of all sixth graders attended the activities fair in September, and of those who did attend, less than half joined any club.

"The right to attend JFK Middle School goes hand in hand with certain responsibilities. Responsibilities to study, to obey school rules, to support school activities. There won't *be* any school activities unless we, the students, support them. No sports." Blaine nodded at Jason. "No Environmental Action Club." She nodded at Dinah. "No drama or music, no science fair, no school newspaper.

"Our school is named after the thirty-fifth president of the United States, John Fitzgerald Kennedy. In his inaugural address, Kennedy said, 'Ask not what your country can do for you; ask what you can do for your country.' I say, 'Ask not what your school can do for you, but what you can do for your school.' Get involved. Join a club. Try out for a team. Make a difference. All of us working together can make JFK the best school in the state. I'm ready. Are you?"

Blaine sat down. It was all Dinah could do not to burst into applause herself. Blaine made Dinah feel proud she had joined the Drama Club, guilty she hadn't joined the Environmental Action Club, sorry she had ever made fun of the Girls' Athletic Association. *Ask not what your school can do for you; ask what you can do for your school.* Dinah could have used a line like that herself: Ask not what your planet can do for you; ask what you can do for your planet.

"Seabrooke. Earth to Dinah Seabrooke," Dixon called out.

Dinah jumped. It was her turn. She walked slowly to the same spot where Jason and Blaine had stood. Then she began.

"I stand before you today as the only candidate for sixth-grade president who will bring a recycling program to your school. Every person in this country throws away four hundred and eighty-one pounds of paper every year. Every day in this country, thousands of trees are chopped down to make paper, thousands of living, breathing, growing trees. Every day more acres of land become a landfill—a garbage dump, crammed full of waste that could have been recycled, that *should* have been recycled.

"The average school throws away tons of paper every year. On Monday I collected ten whole trash bags full of paper other kids had thrown away.

"Look," Dinah said. "Look around you. Lie down on the grass under a tree and look up at its branches. In spring they're covered with fragrant flowers; in summer with cool, green leaves; in autumn with fiery foliage; in winter with soft, white snow. It makes me sick to think of cutting down a beautiful, magnificent tree to make a bunch of Dittos." Scattered applause. "A tree is like a poem. Or a prayer. Or a symphony. It deserves to be saved, and loved.

"We have a chance to keep our planet green and growing. We can chop down more trees and dig more landfills, or we can save trees and recycle. The choice is ours. The choice, this Friday, is yours."

If that didn't make them want to save trees—and vote for Dinah— nothing on earth possibly could.

"Rebuttals. Winfield, two minutes."

Jason faced the class. "I don't really disagree with anything Blaine said. Nobody's more involved in school activities than I am. But I can't go along with Dinah's big thing about saving trees. First of all, even if we recycled paper, nobody else does. If there're a million schools, and one recycles paper and the rest don't, I don't see how that helps anything. Besides, that's what trees are *for*—to use to make things people need. As far as I'm concerned, recycling is a dumb waste of time. About as dumb as wearing a bucket on your head to the cafeteria."

Jason grinned at Dinah. She made herself wait for her turn to reply.

"Yarborough."

"Jason tells us that *he's* involved in school activities. Good. I congratulate him for setting that example. But we need a president who's not only involved himself but will try to get others involved, too. And I want to see kids getting involved not just in sports, but in every school activity.

"Including recycling. Recycling is *not* dumb. I think Dinah's absolutely right about the need for a recycling program in our school. I would have made it part of my platform, except, well, Dinah thought of it first, so it belongs to her. But if I win, I will work to set up a program like Dinah talked about. *We* can do what's right even if everybody else doesn't."

"Seabrooke."

Dinah leaped to her feet, still as furious as she had been two minutes ago.

"What's dumb isn't wearing a bucket on your head. What's dumb is laughing at someone who's trying to make a difference. What's dumb is littering, and throwing away things that could be recycled, and cutting down trees instead of planting new ones. What's dumb is not even noticing that we've just been given one planet, and one chance to take care of it."

Dinah struggled to pull herself together. She wanted to say something as nice about Blaine's speech as Blaine had about hers. She took a deep breath and went on.

"Blaine is right. We *can* make a difference, in all kinds of ways we don't even dream about. Blaine's right that we should ask what we can do for our school. And what we can do for our school is set up a recycling program. What we can do for our planet is save it."

Dinah sat down. Her hands were shaking and she felt close to tears. But she had said what she wanted to say.

"Class. Questions. One at a time. Levine."

"This is for Blaine. I mean, it sounds good to get people involved in school activities, but how are you actually going to do it?"

Blaine had her answer ready. "I have a couple of ideas. One is that I think a different activity should be featured every week on morning announcements. That same week there can be a display all about that activity on the bulletin board in front of the main office. The school newspaper can print more stories about some of the clubs kids don't know much about, instead of writing all the time about sports. And sometimes kids should get out of class to work on a club activity. Everybody wants to get out of class, right?"

The others laughed. Then Mr. Dixon called on the next kid. "Foster."

"This is for Jason. Can you give us any specific example to show how being in sports has given you leadership experience?" Alex Foster was a friend of Jason's; they had obviously planned the question together.

"Good question," Jason said. "Here's one. When I was captain of my baseball team last year, the coach and I had to make decisions about which kids would get to play and which kids would have to sit on the bench. Sometimes good friends of mine ended up sitting on the bench, but I couldn't let them play just because they were my friends. I had to do what was best for the team. If I were president of our class, it would be the same way. I'd do what was best for everybody."

"Adams."

"This is for Dinah." The smirk on Artie's face gave the question away before he even asked it. "In general, do you like to wear strange things on your head?"

"Let's not waste time with jokes, Adams," Mr. Dixon warned.

"Okay, I have another question. Dinah, is it true you love trees so much you want to marry one?"

"Okay, Adams, out of here. One chance is all I give."

Artie cheerfully collected his things and left for Mr. Roemer's office. But the damage was already done. Dinah felt her cheeks flaming. She'd certainly rather marry a tree than a boy.

"Does anyone have a *serious* question for Dinah?"

One girl put up her hand. "Do you really think you can get the school administration to adopt a recycling program?"

"Mr. Roemer told me himself that if one of the new officers took the initiative for a recycling program, he'd look into it."

It was a good answer. But Dinah could tell most kids weren't listening. From somewhere in the back of the room she heard again the familiar chant, "Dinah's in the garbage can, waiting to be collected!"

There were a few other questions, all for Blaine and Jason. Then Mr. Dixon rapped on his desk again. "That's it for today, folks. With the exception of our dear departed friend, Mr. Adams, you came up with some great questions. In the last U.S. presidential election, less than half of the eligible voters chose to exercise their right to vote. I hope all of you vote on Friday. It's up to you to choose one of these three candidates to lead your class through this academic year."

Silently he tapped the pointer against each of the three names he had written on the chalkboard at the beginning of the class period.

Winfield.

Yarborough.

Seabrooke.

"Which one will it be?"

From
You Mean I Have To Stand Up And Say Something?

by Joan Detz
illustrated by David Garner

How to Figure Out What You Want to Say

Okay, you've just gotten an assignment to give a five-to-ten minute speech in English class next Friday.

Now what do you do? Do you race home and start writing your speech? Do you start making lots of charts to illustrate your talk? Do you run to the library to get some facts? No! The first thing you should do is to ask yourself, "What do I really want to say?"

You know, you can't include everything in one speech. If you try to include everything, your audience will become bored and confused.

Do you remember those times when a math teacher tried to put too much material in her lesson and you got confused trying to understand all those complicated formulas?

Or, do you remember when your older brother talked too much at the dinner table and you just wished he'd shut his mouth and give you some peace and quiet?

Well, that's how your audience will feel if you try to put too much stuff in one speech.

So whenever you get a speaking assignment, start by asking yourself, "What do I really want to say?"

Limit yourself to one topic. Don't try to include everything you have ever learned.

For example, suppose you must give a speech about *yourself*. Wow—that's a big topic! You can't possibly tell your audience everything about yourself in five to ten minutes—or even five to ten hours, or five to ten days.

So, start by asking yourself, "Gee, what do I really want to tell these people about me?"

See what I mean? You have *lots* of things to tell people about yourself. Now you must choose the one area that you think will be the most interesting, or the most helpful, or the most unusual.

Remember, if you try to tell the audience everything about yourself, you will just bore them or confuse them—and they won't get a good understanding of who you really are.

Make a list of all the things you could talk about:

- how you love animals and always take care of stray cats and dogs that wander into your neighborhood
- what it was like growing up in a foreign country
- how you got to be so interested in tennis
- the way you always want to try new adventures (camping, backpacking, canoeing—and now a ten-day wilderness hike with your father)
- why you've developed such a good sense of humor

said, "The best time for planning a book is while you're doing the dishes." That can also apply to speeches.

Who knows what wonderful ideas you'll get while you're doing the dishes or making your bed or walking the dog? If it's a good idea, grab it . . . and move on to the next step.

What if you can't think of anything to say?

Can't think of anything to talk about? Don't panic. Just ask yourself, "What's the one subject that always catches my attention? What do I really care about? What topic would I like to hear more about?"

If *you're* interested in the topic of your speech, that enthusiasm will probably rub off on your audience.

Once you get a good idea for a speech, stick with it. *Don't* keep switching topics or trying something else. Commit yourself to that topic, and move ahead with your preparations.

And don't be too fussy about when you get your good ideas. The mystery writer Agatha Christie once

SOURCE

the history magazine for young people
COBBLESTONE
Magazine

A FEW

APPROPRIATE

'REMARKS'

BY

HAROLD HOLTZER

ILLUSTRATED BY

STEPHEN ALCORN

As Union and Confederate forces battled ferociously at Gettysburg, the Union's Commander in Chief, Abraham Lincoln, waited in Washington for news from the front.

Hour after hour during those anxious days and nights, an eyewitness remembered, Lincoln's tall form could be found at the War Department, bent over stacks of telegrams from the battle. On the third day, his burden grew even heavier: His fragile wife, Mary, was thrown from her carriage in a freak accident and suffered a head injury.

Finally, after seventy-two hours of unrelieved tension, Lincoln learned that the North had prevailed at Gettysburg. Privately, he was disappointed that his generals did not follow up their victory by pursuing the Confederates as they fled south. Publicly, he sent the army the "highest honors" for their "great success." He seemed to sense that, flawed or not, the Battle of Gettysburg would be a turning point in the Civil War.

The citizens of Pennsylvania, also aware of their new place in history, moved quickly to create a national cemetery for the thousands of casualties at Gettysburg. A dedication ceremony was planned, and Lincoln received an invitation to attend. He was not, however, asked to deliver the major speech of the day. That

Edward Everett gave a two-hour oratory before Lincoln's speech.

honor was given to a New England statesman and professional orator named Edward Everett. Lincoln, one organizer worried, was incapable of speaking "upon such a great and solemn occasion." The president was asked merely to give "a few appropriate remarks." Yet aware that the event was momentous, Lincoln accepted the halfhearted invitation.

As the day grew near, Lincoln's wife urged him to reconsider. Their young son, Tad, had fallen ill, and Mrs. Lincoln was near hysteria. (Only a year earlier, their middle child, Willie, had died.) On the morning of his father's departure, Tad was so sick he could not eat breakfast. Lincoln himself felt unwell, but he decided to go anyway. With little fanfare, he boarded a train for the slow journey to Gettysburg.

The legend that the president waited until he was on the train to prepare his speech and then scribbled it on the back of an envelope is untrue. Lincoln carefully wrote at least one version of his speech on White House stationery before he left and probably rewrote it in his bedroom in Gettysburg the night before delivering it.

On Thursday, November 19, a balmy, Indian summer day, the six-feet-four Lincoln mounted an

Lincoln rides to the cemetery on an undersized horse.

undersized horse and joined a mournful procession through the town and toward the new cemetery near the battlefield. An immense throng had gathered there, and as Lincoln arrived on the speakers' platform, every man in the crowd respectfully removed his hat. The president was greeted with "a perfect silence."

For two hours, Edward Everett held the spectators spellbound with his rich voice and soaring words. A hymn followed, then Lincoln rose to speak. "Four score and seven years ago," Lincoln began in a high-pitched voice. He spoke for barely three minutes, ending with the words "government of the people, by the people, for the people, shall not perish from the earth."

Almost as soon as he had begun, he sat down. Some eyewitnesses recalled a smattering of applause, but others heard "not a word, not a cheer, not a shout." A stenographer leaned over to Lincoln and asked, "Is that all?" Embarrassed, Lincoln replied, "Yes—for the present." A photographer in the crowd, fussing with his camera, had not even had time to take a picture.

Lincoln thought his speech was a failure. "People are disappointed," he grimly told the man who had introduced him. To add to his misery, he came down with a mild case of smallpox on the trip back to Washington.

Lincoln addresses the crowd at Gettysburg.

Many who listened to the speech felt differently, however. While some newspapers dismissed the speech as "silly," "dull," and "commonplace," another correctly predicted the Gettysburg Address would "live among the annals of man." Perhaps the best compliment of all came from Edward Everett. A few days after they both had spoken at Gettysburg, he wrote to Lincoln, saying he wished he had come "as close to the central idea of the occasion, in two hours, as you did in two minutes." Lincoln replied, telling Everett how pleased he was that "the little I did say was not entirely a failure."

Today, one hundred twenty-five years later, Abraham Lincoln's Gettysburg Address is remembered as one of the great speeches of all time.

Address Delivered at the Dedication of the Cemetery at Gettysburg

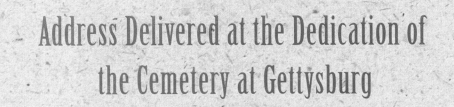

Four score and seven years ago our fathers brought forth on this continent, a new nation, conceived in liberty, and dedicated to the proposition that all men are created equal.

Now we are engaged in a great civil war, testing whether that nation or any nation so conceived, and so dedicated, can long endure. We are met on a great battle field of that war. We have come to dedicate a portion of that field, as a final resting place for those who here gave their lives, that that nation might live. It is altogether fitting and proper that we should do this.

But, in a larger sense, we can not dedicate—we can not consecrate—we can not hallow—this ground. The brave men, living and dead, who struggled here, have consecrated it, far above our poor power to add or detract. The world will little note, nor long remember what we say here, but it can never forget what they did here. It is for us the living, rather, to be dedicated here to the unfinished work which they who fought here have thus far so nobly advanced. It is rather for us to be here dedicated to the great task remaining before us—that from these honored dead we take increased devotion to that cause for which they gave the last full measure of devotion—that we here highly resolve that these dead shall not have died in vain—that this nation, under God, shall have a new birth of freedom—and that government of the people, by the people, for the people, shall not perish from the earth.

Abraham Lincoln
November 19, 1863

History Preserved

President Lincoln hand wrote and autographed a total of five copies of his Gettysburg Address. Photographed here is one of two copies that historian George Bancroft requested from Lincoln. Bancroft had the copies reproduced for the Soldiers' and Sailors' Fair held in Baltimore, MD, in April, 1864. This copy is the best preserved of the five existing handwritten copies.

Four score and seven years ago our fathers brought forth, on this continent, a new nation, conceived in Liberty, and dedicated to the proposition that all men are created equal.

Now we are engaged in a great civil war, testing whether that nation, or any nation so conceived, and so dedicated, can long endure. We are met on a great battle-field of that war. We have come to dedicate a portion of that field, as a final resting-place for those who here gave their lives, that that nation might live. It is altogether fitting and proper that we should do this.

But, in a larger sense, we can not dedicate— we can not consecrate— we can not hallow— this ground. The brave men, living and dead, who struggled here, have consecrated it, far above our poor power to add or detract. The world will little note, nor long remember what we say here, but it can never forget what they did here. It is for us the living, rather, to be dedicated here to the unfinished work which they who fought here have thus far so nobly advanced. It is rather for us to be here dedicated to the great task remaining be-

fore us— that from these honored dead we take in=
creased devotion to that cause for which they here gave
the last full measure of devotion— that we here high=
ly resolve that these dead shall not have died in
vain— that this nation, under God, shall have
a new birth of freedom— and that government
of the people, by the people, for the people, shall
not perish from the earth.

Portrait of Abraham
Lincoln by Matthew Brady,
circa 1862

WORDS That Made HISTORY

Throughout **history, some words have been so powerful that they've changed the way people** think or act. Other speeches have simply moved people with their eloquence. This time line is an overview of some moments in the history of speechmaking that may never be forgotten.

1775 *"Give me liberty, or give me death!"* Revolutionary War hero **Patrick Henry's** famous statement helped convince colonists to fight in the American war for independence.

1848

"We hold these truths to be self-evident: that all men and women *are created equal."* **Elizabeth Cady Stanton** stirred the crowd at the first women's rights convention by reading her own version of the Declaration of Independence.

1851 *"This man...says that women need to be helped into carriages, and lifted over ditches, and to have the best place everywhere. Nobody ever helps me into carriages, or over mud puddles, or gives me the best place, and ain't I a woman?...I have plowed, and planted, and gathered into barns, and no man could help me...and ain't I a woman?"*

A former slave named **Sojourner Truth** was a passionate speaker on the issue of equal rights for women and all African Americans.

1855 *"What is man without the beasts? If all the beasts are gone, men would die from great loneliness of spirit, for whatever happens to*

the beasts also happens to the man." As settlers moved across the United States, they forced Native Americans off of their lands. When **Chief Seattle** surrendered his tribe's lands, he spoke about the different ways that Native Americans and the settlers showed their respect for the earth.

1912

"I shall ask you to be as quiet as possible. I don't know whether you fully understand that I have just been shot; but it takes more than that to kill a Bull Moose."
Teddy Roosevelt was campaigning for president as the Bull Moose candidate when he delivered a death-defying speech. As Roosevelt was about to begin speaking, a man stepped out of the crowd and shot him in the chest. That didn't stop Roosevelt! He insisted on giving his speech before agreeing to go to a hospital.

1961

"And so my fellow Americans, ask not what your country can do for you; ask what you can do for your country."
John F. Kennedy gave an inaugural speech in which his words made an impact on the mood of the entire country. Kennedy wanted people to understand what it meant to be an American citizen.

1963

"I have a dream that my four little children will one day live in a country where they will not be judged by the color of their skin but by the content of their character."
These words from **Martin Luther King, Jr.'s** famous speech at the civil rights March on Washington expressed hope for a better future for everyone.

1969

"That's one small step for a man; one giant leap for mankind." **Astronaut Neil Armstrong** spoke these famous words after taking the first step ever on the moon!

1991

"As female students today, your challenges will come not so much in breaking new paths — as your mothers, grandmothers and I have done — but in deciding which to choose among the many paths now open to you." When **Sandra Day O'Connor** became the first woman justice appointed to the U.S. Supreme Court she became an inspiration to many young women, including the graduates she addressed at Widener University.

1993

"Here on the pulse of this new day/You may have the grace to look up and out/And into your sister's eyes, /And into your brother's face, /Your country, / And say simply/With hope — /Good morning." **Maya Angelou** composed a poem, "On the Pulse of the Morning" for President Bill Clinton's inauguration. Millions watched on television as she read.

How to
Give a Stage Presentation

It's your turn to be in the spotlight!

"All the world's a stage," wrote the famous playwright William Shakespeare. Though you may not be a performer, you'll probably be called "on stage" at some time in your life. You might have to make a speech or give an oral report. Here's an opportunity to give a stage presentation about something you know well or really care about. The format you choose for your presentation might be a monologue, a report, a speech, or a song.

Be expressive.

Make eye contact

Smile

Wait for laughs

Choose Your Topic and Format

Begin by deciding what you want your presentation to be about. Aim for a presentation that's about five to ten minutes long. That can seem like a long time when you're on stage by yourself, so be sure the topic you pick is something you're interested in! You might want to focus on something happening in the news. Or you might choose to focus on a hobby, a person who inspires you, or something you consider yourself an expert in.

Once you have picked your topic, think creatively about the best way to get your message across. For example, if your topic is a hot news story, you might deliver the information as if you were a newscaster.

If telling jokes is your hobby, you may want to organize a comedy routine. Here are some additional ideas for formats for your presentation. Can you think of any others?

- song
- oral report
- poem
- speech

TOOLS

- Paper and a pencil
- Props, costumes, and sound effects

2 Write Your Script

Whatever your presentation is, you'll need to write a script for it. If you're creating your own monologue or comedy routine, or reading some of your own poems, you'll need to spend some time writing and organizing your material. If you're giving a report or a speech on a favorite topic, you'll need to write out what you'll say.

You might want to outline the main points you'll cover first and then fill in the details.

How Am I Doing?

Before you stage your presentation, take a few minutes to ask yourself these questions:

- **Did I choose a topic that interests me and suits my audience?**

- **Do I know (or can I find out) 5–10 minutes worth of pertinent information about my topic?**

- **Have I chosen an appropriate format for my topic and audience?**

Tip You might want to reread "You Mean I Have to Stand Up and Say Something?" in this SourceBook for advice on how to choose a topic.

Scholastic 0-590-45828-0 / $1.95

The Abraham Lincoln Joke Book

By
Beatrice Schenk de Regniers

Illustrations by
William Lahey Cummings

3 Prepare Your Presentation

It takes more than a good script to give your presentation pizzazz. If you did the storytelling workshop, you've learned how to make a presentation exciting. Think about using props, costumes, music, or visual aids to spice up your act. Mark up your script with any ideas you want to include.

Your presentation will be most successful if it's well-rehearsed. Have a friend or family member observe a rehearsal. They can tell you whether you're speaking clearly, and whether your props and other devices make sense to the audience. Refer to your script when you need to, but try to rely on it less the more you practice.

If You Are Using A Computer

Use the Sign format on your computer to make programs and banners for the performance. Illustrate them with clip-art or create your own drawings.

4 Stage Your Performance

Here are some suggestions for making your presentation a success.

- Monitor your voice. Speak loudly and clearly so that even the people in the back can hear you. To help your voice carry, keep your head up and try to face the audience.

- Use body language. Your gestures help to create drama and excitement! Move your face, hands, and body in ways that reinforce what you are saying.

- Organize your material so that the presentation goes smoothly.

- Finally, you might invite a parent or your school media specialist to videotape your presentation. You can watch the tape afterward and evaluate your performance.

CONGRATULATIONS

Now you know what it's like to share your creative voice with an audience. You'll use your creativity in many different situations.

José García
Drama Coach

127

Glossary

ap•plause (a plôz´) *noun*
A way of showing appreciation for something, especially by clapping.

applause

au•di•ence
(ô´ dē əns) *noun*
A group of people who have gathered to watch a play, speech, or other public performance.

bal•lads
(bal´əds) *noun*
Simple poems or stories that tell a song in short verses. ▲ **ballad**

cam•paign
(kam pān´) *noun*
A series of planned actions taken to reach a goal.

chant (chant) *noun*
A manner of singing or speaking in a musical monotone.

can•di•dates
(kan´ di dāts´) *noun*
People who seek a particular position or high honor. All *candidates* for class president must give speeches. ▲ **candidate**

cau•ses (kô´ zəz) *noun*
Ideas or principles that people actively support. ▲ **cause**

coach (kōch) *noun*
A person who trains or instructs performers.

con•ven•tion
(kən ven´shən) *noun*
A group of people who get together to discuss a particular idea or belief.

de•but
(dā byo͞o´) *noun*
A first public appearance by a performer.

audience

ded·i·ca·tion
(ded´i kā´shən) *noun*
The act of setting aside for
a special purpose.

dra·mat·i·cal·ly
(drə ma´ tik lē´) *adverb*
Vividly, in an exciting or
suspenseful way.

el·o·quence
(el´ə kwens) *noun*
The ability to speak in a
way that stirs people's
emotions.

Word History

The word **eloquence** comes
from the Latin word
eloquens meaning "to
put into words."

eye·wit·ness
(ī´wit´nis) *noun*
A person who sees an act
or event and can give a
firsthand account of it.

fas·ci·nat·ed
(fas´ ə nā´ təd) *verb*
Captured the interest of.
▲ **fascinate**

folk tales
(fōk tāls) *noun*
Stories that were passed
along by word of mouth
before being written down.
▲ **folk tale**

im·pressed
(im prest´) *adjective*
Positively influenced or
affected. Having a strong,
positive opinion of.

in·ci·dent
(in´ si dənt) *noun*
A distinct event or piece of
action, as in a story. John
told me about a funny
incident that happened on
the school playground.

Thesaurus

incident
episode
event
occurrence

lime·light
(līm´ līt´) *noun*
The center of public
attention.

Fact File

The *lime* in **limelight** isn't
the kind you pick off a tree.
It's a chemical substance
that, when heated, gives off
a brilliant white light.
Scottish inventor Thomas
Drummond, born in 1797,
used lime to create a
lighting device that was
later used to illuminate
lighthouses and, eventually,
theatrical stages.

a	add	o͝o	took	ə =	
ā	ace	o͞o	pool	ə in *above*	
â	care	u	up	e in *sicken*	
ä	palm	û	burn	i in *possible*	
e	end	yo͞o	fuse	o in *melon*	
ē	equal	oi	oil	u in *circus*	
i	it	ou	pout		
ī	ice	ng	ring		
o	odd	th	thin		
ō	open	th	this		
ô	order	zh	vision		

Glossary

me·mo·ri·al
(mə môr′ē əl) *noun*
Something designed to keep a memory alive; a monument.

mon·u·ment
(mon′yə mənt) *noun*
A structure that commemorates a person or event.

Word History

The word **monument** is from the Latin word *monumentum* meaning "to remind."

mused
(myo͞ozd) *verb*
Said with extended or contemplative thought. Ellen *mused* about why her sister seemed so sad.
▲ **muse**

or·a·tor (ôr′ ə tər) *noun*
A person who is known to be a good public speaker.

Fact File

One of the most famous **orators** of all time was Roman statesman Mark Antony. The funeral speech, or *oration*, he made for Julius Caesar is considered to be a masterpiece, and is still quoted today.

orator

pan·to·mime
(pan′ tə mīm′) *noun*
A performance in which a story is told through movement and gestures, not words.

Word History

The word **pantomime** comes from two Greek words, *panto*, meaning "all," and *mimos*, meaning "imitator." Panto + mime = someone who can imitate anything.

plat·form
(plat′ fôrm) *noun*
Ideas and causes adopted by a person running for political office.

poll (pōl) *noun*
A record of people's opinions or votes on a given subject.

pre·serv·ing
(pri zûrv′ing) *verb*
Keeping safe; maintaining.
▲ **preserve**

pre·view
(prē′ vyo͞o′) *noun*
An early showing or performance.

pro·duc·er
(prə do͞o′ sər) *noun*
The person who raises the money for a performance.

pro·jec·tions
(prə jek′ shənz) *noun*
Pictures or images that appear on a screen.
▲ **projection**

pub·lic·ly
(pub′ lik lē) *adverb*
In a public or open manner or place.

pub·lic·i·ty stunt
(pu blis′ i tē stunt) *noun*
An event staged to gain public attention for a person or thing.

re·but·tals
(ri but′ lz) *noun*
Answers that disagree with what has been said. After your opponents have stated their opinions, you will have time to make your *rebuttals.* ▲ **rebuttal**

Thesaurus

rebuttal
comeback
response
retort

re·hears·al
(ri hûr′ səl) *noun*
A practice run of a performance, speech, play, or other public program.

spell·bound
(spel′ bound′) *adjective*
Fascinated or enchanted by something.

spot·light
(spot′ līt′) *noun*
Strong beam of light used to highlight performers on stage.

Word Study

The word **spotlight** can also mean "to make conspicuous; to draw attention to."

sym·bol·ic
(sim bol′ ik) *adjective*
Serving as a sign or representation of something.

the·at·ri·cal
(thē a′ tri kəl) *adjective*
Of or pertaining to dramatic presentations.

throng (thrông) *noun*
A large number of people crowded together.

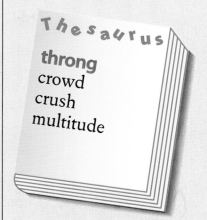

Thesaurus

throng
crowd
crush
multitude

tra·di·tion·al
(trə dish′ ə nl) *adjective*
Relating to beliefs and customs passed from one generation to the next by word of mouth or by example.

a	add	o͝o	took	ə =
ā	ace	o͞o	pool	a in *above*
â	care	u	up	e in *sicken*
ä	palm	û	burn	i in *possible*
e	end	yo͞o	fuse	o in *melon*
ē	equal	oi	oil	u in *circus*
i	it	ou	pout	
ī	ice	ng	ring	
o	odd	th	thin	
ō	open	ŧh	this	
ô	order	zh	vision	

Authors & Illustrators

Floyd Cooper *pages 10–35*

This award-winning illustrator is known for expressive paintings that seem to draw the reader into the characters' worlds. The paintings in *From Miss Ida's Porch* were inspired by Floyd Cooper's childhood memories of neighborhood storytelling.

Myra Cohn Livingston *pages 60–61*

Today, she is one of the best-known writers of children's poetry, but Myra Cohn Livingston began her career as a professional musician. Now she creates music with words. "I think poetry must have music," Livingston says. She has composed hundreds of poems on subjects including animals, ocean life, and outer space.

Claudia Mills *pages 90–105*

This author published her first novel for young readers in 1981, but she began writing as a child. At fourteen, Claudia Mills wrote her autobiography. Called *T Is for Tarzan*, it was a big hit at her junior high school. Today, Mills lives in Maryland, where she is a college professor.

José Ortega *pages 52–59*

Born in Ecuador, this illustrator moved to New York City when he was five. José Ortega says he has always loved to draw. After high school, he attended the School of Visual Arts and became a professional artist. When illustrating "La Bamba," Ortega tried to match Gary Soto's humorous story twists in his drawings, which he created on a computer.

Gary Soto *pages 52–59*

This author says that his childhood inspired a great deal of his poems, short stories, and novels. Gary Soto has vivid memories of growing up in a predominantly Mexican-American neighborhood in Fresno, California. While attending college, Soto discovered poetry. He decided to become a writer and began putting the stories in his head down on paper. Soto hopes his work will inspire his readers the way other writers have inspired him.

Laurence Yep *pages 36–43*

Born in San Francisco, this author grew up reading science-fiction and fantasy stories. When he first started writing children's books, he began with these genres. Later, Laurence Yep explored folk tales from his Chinese heritage. Yep has won numerous awards, including the Newbery Honor Book award for *Dragonwings*.

Books &

More by Laurence Yep

Dragonwings
It's the early 1900s and Moonshadow has just come to San Francisco from China to live with his father. Read about his experiences in his new home.

The Lost Garden
Here, Laurence Yep tells the story of his own life. Find out how the writer got his start.

Tongues of Jade
In this collection, master storyteller Laurence Yep retells 17 Chinese-American tales.

Laurence Yep

Dynamite Dinah
by Claudia Mills
Dinah's new baby brother is monopolizing her parents' attention and her best friend has won the lead role in the school play. What can Dinah do to make her feel like a star again?

Radio Fifth Grade
by Gordon Korman
Benjy is the disc jockey for Kidsview, the fifth grade's school radio show, and he's determined to do everything he can to make people listen!

Thank You, Dr. Martin Luther King, Jr.
by Eleanora Tate
When two storytellers visit her school, Mary Elouise discovers that performing is one way to proclaim her pride in herself and her African-American heritage.

Bard of Avon: The Story of William Shakespeare
by Diane Stanley and Peter Vennema
The great playwright and his times are brought to life in words and pictures in this lively biography.

Sojourner Truth: Ain't I a Woman?
by Patricia and Fredrick McKissack
The courageous and eloquent Sojourner Truth spoke out in the fight to abolish slavery, and later became a pioneer women's-rights activist.

Theater Magic: Behind the Scenes at a Children's Theater
by Cheryl Walsh Bellville
Learning lines, building sets, sewing costumes— so many things go into putting on a stage production! This photo essay traces the process from start to finish, using an actual production of *The Nightingale* as a model.

&Media

Videos

The Girl Who Spelled Freedom
Disney

Based on a true story, this video focuses on a family who leaves Cambodia to begin a new life in America. As their daughter begins to learn English, she develops a passion for spelling that leads her to win an important spelling bee. (90 minutes)

Voices of Sarafina
PBS/Pacific Arts Video

This documentary tells the story of a group of young South Africans who performed in a powerful anti-apartheid musical. (60 minutes)

Software

Storyteller
Multimeanings
(IBM CD-ROM)

Storytellers can help pass on their cultural histories. This interactive video includes music, games, and lots of information. Choose the language you want to use: English or Spanish.

Video Jam
EA Kids
(Mac, IBM)

Choose from over 50 musical works, a variety of characters, special effects, and background scenes, to create your very own music videos.

Magazines

Plays
Plays

This magazine is a source for all kinds of plays suitable for classroom and school productions.

Storyworks
Scholastic Inc.

This entertaining magazine includes stories and interviews, and has a play in every issue!

A Place to Write

**Toastmasters International
2200 North Grand Avenue
Santa Ana, CA 92711**

Write for information about a program that can help you become a better public speaker.

Acknowledgments

Grateful acknowledgment is made to the following sources for permission to reprint from previously published material. The publisher has made diligent efforts to trace the ownership of all copyrighted material in this volume and believes that all necessary permissions have been secured. If any errors or omissions have inadvertently been made, proper corrections will gladly be made in future editions.

Cover: Illustration of "Doug®" copyright © 1993 Viacom International, Inc. All rights reserved. "Doug®" and all related titles and characters are trademarks of Viacom International, Inc. Used by permission.

Interior: "From Miss Ida's Porch" from FROM MISS IDA'S PORCH by Sandra Belton with illustrations by Floyd Cooper. Text copyright © 1993 by Sandra Belton. Illustrations copyright © 1993 by Floyd Cooper. Reprinted by arrangement with Simon & Schuster Books for Young Readers, Simon & Schuster Children's Publishing Division.

"The Homecoming" and cover from THE RAINBOW PEOPLE by Laurence Yep. Text copyright © 1989 by Laurence Yep. Reprinted by permission of HarperCollins Publishers.

The cover of the brochure from the National Storytelling Festival is used by the kind permission of the National Storytelling Association, Jonesborough, TN 37659.

"How the Coyote Gets His Name" by Jerry Tello is now available under the title COYOTE, HOW HE GETS HIS NAME by Jerry Tello. Copyright © 1993 by Jerry Tello. Published by Sueños Publications. Notes are used by permission of the author.

"La Bamba" from BASEBALL IN APRIL AND OTHER STORIES by Gary Soto. Copyright © 1990 by Gary Soto. Reprinted by permission of Harcourt Brace & Company. Book cover illustration by Barry Root, copyright © 1990 by Barry Root. Reprinted by permission of the illustrator. "La Bamba" (Ritchie Valens) copyright © 1958 Picture Our Music. Administered by Warner-Tamerlane Publishing Corp. All rights reserved.

"School Play" from REMEMBERING AND OTHER POEMS by Myra Cohn Livingston. Copyright © 1989 by Myra Cohn Livingston. Reprinted by arrangement with Margaret K. McElderry Books, Simon & Schuster Children's Publishing Division. Cover illustration by Neil Waldman. Illustration copyright © 1989 by Neil Waldman. Reprinted by permission of the artist.

"Doug Can't Dig It" television script from Nickelodeon/MTV Networks. Text and illustrations from Jumbo Pictures, copyright © 1993 Viacom International, Inc. All rights reserved. "Doug" is a registered trademark of Viacom International, Inc., "Doug®" and all related titles and characters are trademarks of Viacom International, Inc. Used by permission.

Selection from an adaptation from "Vanessa's Bad Grade," an episode of the NBC-TV series *The Cosby Show*. Written by Ross Brown. A Carsey-Werner Production in association with Bill Cosby. Copyright © 1985. Used by permission. All rights reserved. Adaptation originally printed in *Scholastic SCOPE®* magazine, Volume 36, No. 4, October 2, 1987.

Selection and cover from DINAH FOR PRESIDENT by Claudia Mills. Text copyright © 1992 by Claudia Mills. This edition is reprinted by arrangement with Simon & Schuster Books for Young Readers, Simon & Schuster Children's Publishing Division. Cover illustration by Eileen McKeating copyright © 1992 by Eileen McKeating. Reprinted by permission of the artist.

Selection and cover from YOU MEAN I HAVE TO STAND UP AND SAY SOMETHING? by Joan Detz. Text copyright © 1986 by Joan Detz. Cover illustration copyright © 1986 by David Marshall. Reprinted by permission of PMA Literary Agency & Film Management for the authors.

"A Few Appropriate Remarks" from *Cobblestone*'s July 1988 issue: "The Battle of Gettysburg," copyright © 1988, Cobblestone Publishing, Inc., 7 School Street, Peterborough, NH 03458. Reprinted by permission of the publisher. Cobblestone logo is a registered trademark of Cobblestone Publishing, Inc. Used by permission.

Cover illustration by William Lahey Cummings from THE ABRAHAM LINCOLN JOKE BOOK by Beatrice Schenk de Regniers. Illustrations © 1965. Reprinted by permission of Scholastic Inc. Cover illustration by Joyce Behr from HUMOROUS MONOLOGUES by Martha Bolton. Copyright © 1989 by Martha Bolton. All rights reserved. Originally published by Sterling Publishing Co., Inc. Used by permission of Martha Bolton. "Dinosaurs" from *Scholastic News®*, March 3, 1995. Copyright © 1995. Published by Scholastic Inc. Used by permission.

Cover from DEAR DR. BELL . . . YOUR FRIEND, HELEN KELLER by Judith St. George. Illustration copyright © 1992 by G. P. Putnam's Sons. Published by G. P. Putnam's Sons, a division of The Putnam & Grosset Group.

Cover from KOYA DELANEY AND THE GOOD GIRL BLUES by Eloise Greenfield, illustrated by Jan Spivey Gilchrist. Illustration copyright © 1992 by Jan Spivey Gilchrist. Published by Scholastic Inc.

Cover from SCHOOL SPIRIT by Johanna Hurwitz, illustrated by Liana Somana. Published by William Morrow & Company, Inc. Illustration copyright © 1995 by Scholastic Inc.

Cover from THAT'S A WRAP!: HOW MOVIES ARE MADE by Ned Dowd, photograph by Henry Horenstein. Photograph copyright © 1991 by Henry Horenstein. Published by Simon & Schuster Books for Young Readers, Simon & Schuster Children's Publishing Division.

Photography and Illustration Credits

Photos: © John Lei for Scholastic Inc. all Tool Box items unless otherwise noted. p. 2: © Valerie Santagto for Scholastic Inc. pp. 2-3 background: © Valerie Santagto for Scholastic Inc. p. 3 br: © Valerie Santagto for Scholastic Inc.; tc: © Maxwell MacKenzie/Tony Stone Images. p. 4 c: © Ana Esperanza Nance for Scholastic Inc.; tc: © Maxwell MacKenzie/Tony Stone Images. p. 5 c: © Lee F. Snyder/Photo Researchers, Inc.; tc: © Maxwell MacKenzie/Tony Stone Images. p. 6 c: © Michael Newman/PhotoEdit; tc: © Maxwell MacKenzie/Tony Stone Images. p. 44 tc: © Larry Maglott for Scholastic Inc.; c, bc: © Tom Raymond/Fresh Air Photographics. p. 46 br: © Jerry Jacka/Courtesy Gallery 10. bl: © Chris Marona/Photo Researchers, Inc. p. 47 br: © David McGlynn/FPG International Corp. p. 48 bc: © Stanley Bach for Scholastic Inc. p. 49 tr: © John Lei for Scholastic Inc.; bl: © Stanley Bach for Scholastic Inc.; br: © Valerie Santagto for Scholastic Inc. p. 80 c: © Maxwell MacKenzie/Tony Stone Images, Inc.; all others: © Valerie Santagto for Scholastic Inc. pp. 80-81 c: © Valerie Santagto for Scholastic Inc. pp. 81-83: © Valerie Santagto for Scholastic Inc. p. 84 © Photo Courtesy of NBC. p. 86 br, bc: © Stanley Bach for Scholastic Inc. p. 87 br: © Valerie Santagto for Scholastic Inc. p. 112 cl: © Brown Brothers. p. 114 tc: © Stock Montage, Inc. pp. 116-117 c: Courtesy of the Division of Rare and Manuscript Collections, Cornell University Library. pp. 118-121 border: © Joe Sohm/The Image Works. p. 119 tr: © FPG International Corp.; tl, cr: © The Granger Collection; bc: © National Museum of the American Indian. p. 120 tr: © Brown Brothers; cl: © Stanley Tretick/Sygma; br: © Bob Adelman/Magnum Photos. p. 121 tr: © J. Tiziou/Sygma; c: © O. Franken/Sygma; br: © Wally McNamee/Sygma. pp. 122-123 c, tc: © John Lei for Scholastic Inc. p. 123 c: © Stanley Bach for Scholastic Inc. p. 124 bc: © Stanley Bach for Scholastic Inc.; br: © John Lei for Scholastic Inc. p. 125 bl: © John Lei for Scholastic Inc.; tr: © Stanley Bach for Scholastic Inc. p. 126 tr: © Stanley Bach for Scholastic Inc.; br: © John Lei for Scholastic Inc. p. 127 c: © John Lei for Scholastic Inc.; cr, bl: © Stanley Bach for Scholastic Inc.; br: © Valerie Santagto for Scholastic Inc.; p. 128 tl, c: © Art Gingert/ Comstock, Inc. p. 130 tc: © Jon Feingersh/The Stock Market. p. 132 tl: Scholastic Photo Library; bl: Diane Guthrie; cl: © Courtesy of Myra Cohn Livingston. p. 133 cr, br: Scholastic Trade Department; tr: Hans Neleman; br: Scholastic Photo Library. p.134 bl: © Courtesy of Scholastic Photo Library. p. 135 br: © Stanley Bach for Scholastic Inc.

Illustrations: pp. 8-9: Keith Bendis; pp. 10, 11, 16, 18, 19, 22, 24, 28, 30, 32, 33: Jans Evans; pp. 33-34, 39, 40, 42-43: Chi Chung; 50-51: Keith Bendis; pp. 53-54, 57-59: José Ortega; pp. 60-61: Curtis Parker; pp. 88-89: Keith Bendis; pp. 90, 93, 97, 100: Michael Steirnagle; pp. 106-109: David Garner; pp. 110-111, 113-115: Stephen Alcorn; pp. 144-148, 150-151: Chi Chung.